First Edition

Maria Wilson

triumphlearning™
Common Core Coach
English Language Arts 8
Assessments

Common Core Coach Assessments, English Language Arts, First Edition, Grade 8
T107NAA

ISBN-13: 978-1-61997-459-3

Cover Design: Q2A/Bill Smith
Cover Illustration: Jing Jing Tsong

Triumph Learning® 136 Madison Avenue, 7th Floor, New York, NY 10016

Contents

Benchmark Assessment

1

Part 1: Reading Comprehension

Read the passage and answer the questions that follow.

Bessie's Show

"Ah-choo!" A young boy sneezed as a strong gust of wind kicked up some dust. He stood in a cow pasture, mesmerized by the plane buzzing overhead. The small Curtiss Jenny plane, which people described as little more than a bunch of parts flying in formation, performed graceful figure eights over an amazed crowd. "Look at Brave Bessie go!" the boy exclaimed to no one in particular.

In the cockpit of the plane, the aviator, Bessie Coleman, laughed in delight as she straightened the plane. The young woman was doing exactly what she had always wanted to do. She was making her living as a barnstormer, which was quite unusual for an African American woman in the 1920s.

Next, Bessie decided to attempt a stall. *Stalls always impress audiences*, she thought. She positioned the plane directly over the crowd and turned off the engine. She imagined the collective gasp of the spectators as they heard the engine go silent, causing the plane to glide at only forty-five miles per hour.

Bessie was low enough to detect expressions of relief as she restarted the engine. A blast of exhaust fumes hit her nostrils and a splat of oil sprayed out as she coaxed her Jenny to reach its top speed of seventy-five miles per hour.

Brave Bessie entertained her admirers with more figure eights, barrel rolls, and dives. Then she prepared for the grand finale, which included a new feat. She had recently spiced up her show with parachute jumps to maintain the interest of her audiences.

Bessie examined the herd of cattle at the far end of the pasture. An advantage of flying over farmland was being able to use cows as weathervanes since the animals turn their tails to the wind. After checking the wind direction, she increased the altitude of the plane. "Ready?" she yelled over the engine's buzz to Eliza Dilworth, who was crammed into the miniature plane with her.

Eliza climbed out of the cockpit and cautiously crept to a large canvas bag, which was tied to the wing with a rope. The wind was strong, knocking off her hat and turning her fingers into icicles, as she tried to grip the wing. The bag contained the parachute that would transport her to the ground. She donned the parachute, sat down on the wing, and jumped. "Snap!" went the rope that had secured the package to the wing. Eliza's parachute billowed open and floated her downward to the ground as the crowd stared in amazement.

The pilot watched with satisfaction and then circled back over the field, scouting for a suitable landing location. She decreased her speed, knowing the importance of coming in very slowly because the Jenny had no brakes.

The plane landed smoothly and chugged safely to a stop. The boy who had been watching Bessie with rapt attention was the first to approach when she jumped out of the plane. His eyes sparkled upon seeing the woman in her aviator outfit. He could not contain his excitement as he blurted out: "I have to learn how to do that! It's the most exciting thing I have ever seen!"

Bessie smiled kindly and replied, "My dream is to start a flight school, but you are a bit too young to take lessons just yet. In the meantime, would you like to go for a ride?" Bessie expected the boy to agree eagerly, but instead he looked very disappointed.

"I don't have the five dollars," he said dejectedly, pointing to the poster advertising the fee for rides.

"What if I take you up for free and you pay me back when you become a famous aviator?" she offered with a twinkle in her eyes.

The boy's face broke into a huge grin as he said, "I'll be right back after I tell my dad where I'm going."

"Watch out," Bessie called after him, laughing. "Once flying is in your blood, it's almost impossible to get it out."

1. Which of the following details from the passage BEST supports the idea that Eliza was on the wing of the plane while it was flying?

   A. "The bag contained the parachute that would transport her to the ground."

   B. "'Ready?' she yelled over the engine's buzz to Eliza Dilworth, who was crammed into the miniature plane with her."

   C. "The pilot watched with satisfaction and then circled back over the field, scouting for a suitable landing location."

   D. "Eliza climbed out of the cockpit and cautiously crept to a large canvas bag, which was tied to the wing with a rope."

2. What is the point of view of the passage?

   A. first person

   B. second person

   C. third person, limited

   D. third person, omniscient

3. What is the theme of the passage?

   A. Friends can help you overcome your fears.

   B. Share what you love with others.

   C. Practice makes perfect.

   D. Don't let anyone stop you from being yourself.

4. Read this sentence from the passage.

   The wind was strong, knocking off her hat and turning her fingers into icicles, as she tried to grip the wing.

   In this sentence, the author is trying to

   A. show readers how Eliza has never jumped with a parachute.

   B. encourage readers to learn to do plane stunts.

   C. cause readers to have a feeling of suspense.

   D. suggest to readers that Bessie doesn't care about Eliza's safety.

5. What is the setting of the passage?

   A. an airport

   B. a flying school

   C. a cow pasture

   D. a small farm

6. Why does Bessie look at the herd of cattle? Use details from the passage to support your answer.

   Bessie looks at the herd of cattle because it is an advantage to her to use cows as weathervanes since the animals turn their tails to the wind.

Read the passage and answer the questions that follow.

excerpted and adapted from

The Hound of the Baskervilles
by Arthur Conan Doyle

Mr. Sherlock Holmes was seated at the breakfast table. I stood upon the hearthrug and picked up the stick that our visitor had left behind him the night before. It was a fine, thick piece of wood. Just under the head was a broad silver band, nearly an inch across. "To James Mortimer, M.R.C.S., from his friends of the C.C.H." was engraved upon it, with the date "1884." It was just such a stick that an old-fashioned family practitioner used to carry—dignified, solid, and reassuring.

"Well, Watson, what do you make of our visitor's stick? Let me hear you <u>reconstruct</u> the man by an examination of it."

"I think," said I, "that Dr. Mortimer is a successful, elderly medical man and well-esteemed since those who know him gave him this mark of their appreciation."

"Good!" said Holmes. "Excellent!"

"I think also that the probability is in favor of his being a country practitioner who does a great deal of his visiting on foot."

"Why so?"

"Because this stick, though originally a very handsome one, has been so knocked about that I can hardly imagine a town practitioner carrying it. The thick iron tip on the bottom is worn down, so it is evident that he has done a great amount of walking with it."

"Perfectly sound!" said Holmes.

"And then again, there is the 'friends of the C.C.H.' I should guess that to be the Something Hunt, the local hunting club, to whose members he has possibly given some surgical assistance and which has made him a small presentation in return."

"Really, Watson, you excel yourself," said Holmes, pushing back his chair. "It may be that you are not yourself luminous, but you are a conductor of light. Some people without possessing genius have a remarkable power of stimulating it."

He had never said as much before. I was proud to think that I had so far mastered his system as to apply it in a way that earned his approval. He now took the stick from my hands. Then, with an expression of interest, he carried the cane to the window and looked it over again with a hand lens.

"Interesting, though elementary," said he as he returned to his favorite corner.

"Has anything escaped me?" I asked with some self-importance.

"I am afraid, my dear Watson, that most of your conclusions were erroneous. When I said that you stimulated me, I meant, to be frank, that in noting your mistakes, I was guided toward the truth. Not that you are entirely wrong. The man is certainly a country practitioner. And he walks a good deal."

"Then I was right."

"To that extent."

"But that was all."

"No, no, my dear Watson, not all—by no means all. I would suggest, for example, that a presentation to a doctor is more likely to come from a hospital than from a hunting club, and that when the initials 'C.C.' are placed before that hospital, the words 'Charing Cross' very naturally suggest themselves."

"You may be right. Supposing that 'C.C.H.' does stand for Charing Cross Hospital, what further inferences may we draw?"

"Do none suggest themselves? You know my methods. Apply them!"

"I can only think of the obvious conclusion that the man has practiced in town before going to the country."

"I think that we might venture a little farther. Look at it in this light: When would his friends unite to give him a gift of their good will? Obviously, at the moment when Dr. Mortimer withdrew from the service of the hospital in order to start a country practice for himself."

"It certainly seems probable."

"Now, you will observe that he could not have been on the staff of the hospital. Only a well-established London doctor could hold such a position, and such a one would not drift into the country. If he was in the hospital and yet not on the staff, then he could only have been a house surgeon—little more than a student. And he left five years ago—the date is on the stick. So, your grave, middle-aged family practitioner vanishes into thin air, my dear Watson, and there emerges a young fellow under thirty, amiable, unambitious, absent-minded, and the possessor of a favorite dog, which I should describe roughly as being larger than a terrier and smaller than a mastiff."

I laughed incredulously as Sherlock Holmes leaned back.

Holmes had a mischievous smile and said, "I think that I am fairly justified in my inferences. As to the adjectives, it is my experience that it is only an amiable man in this world who receives testimonials, only an unambitious one who abandons a London career for the country, and only an absent-minded one who leaves his stick and not his visiting-card after waiting an hour in your room."

"And the dog?"

"Has been in the habit of carrying this stick. The marks of his teeth are plainly visible. The dog's jaw, as shown in the space between these marks, is too broad in my opinion for a terrier and not broad enough for a mastiff. It may have been—yes, by Jove, it is a curly-haired spaniel."

He halted by the window.

"My dear fellow, how can you possibly be so sure?"

"For the very simple reason that I see the dog himself on our very door-step, and there is the ring of its owner. What does Dr. James Mortimer, the man of science, ask of Sherlock Holmes, the specialist in crime? Come in!"

7. Which line of dialogue BEST demonstrates the relationship between Holmes and Watson?

   A. "I am afraid, my dear Watson, that most of your conclusions were erroneous."

   B. "I think that I am fairly justified in my inferences."

   C. "The man is certainly a country practitioner."

   D. "What does Dr. James Mortimer, the man of science, ask of Sherlock Holmes, the specialist in crime?"

8. Which is an example of situational irony in the passage?

   A. Sherlock Holmes looks at the cane closely with his eyes and then with a hand lens.

   B. Sherlock Holmes says that Watson is "a conductor of light" but thinks Watson has made several mistakes.

   C. Watson thinks the 'H' stands for "hunt," but Sherlock Holmes thinks the 'H' stands for "hospital."

   D. Sherlock Holmes knows about the doctor's dog by looking out the room's window.

9. What is the BEST summary of the passage?

   A. Watson looks at the doctor's cane. He thinks that the doctor is a country doctor who walks a lot. Also, he thinks that the cane was a gift.

   B. Sherlock Holmes explains to Watson why he thinks the doctor is young, not old. Also, he explains why he thinks the doctor has a dog.

   C. The doctor left his cane. Watson and Sherlock Holmes draw conclusions about the doctor, based on the cane. Then the doctor returns.

   D. Sherlock Holmes thinks the doctor is young, friendly, absent-minded, and has a dog. But Watson doesn't believe that the doctor has a dog.

10. Read these sentences from the passage.

    "Well, Watson, what do you make of our visitor's stick? Let me hear you reconstruct the man by an examination of it."

    The author uses the word reconstruct to suggest that Watson should

    A. form a mental picture of the doctor.

    B. build a sculpture of the doctor.

    C. use wood to make a new stick.

    D. look outside to find the doctor.

11. What is the point of view of the passage?

    A. first person

    B. second person

    C. third person, limited

    D. third person, omniscient

12. Which word BEST describes Sherlock Holmes and why? Use details from the passage to support your answer.

_____

_____

_____

_____

_____

Read the passage and answer the questions that follow.

Echo and Narcissus
excerpted and adapted from **A Book of Myths**

by Jean Lang

In the solitudes of the hills, we find her. She will answer us where waves lash themselves against rugged cliffs. At nightfall, she mimics the cry of a wailing bird that calls for its mate. She makes the crash of the falling limb of a dead tree go on and on, and she tortures the human being who is lost, hopelessly lost, by repeating his despairing calls for help. But she also echoes the children's voices as they play by the seashore or pick primroses in the woods in spring; and when they greet her with laughter, she laughs in merry response.

Yet, the nymph who sought love and failed must surely find some comfort on those bright days of summer when she gives the little children happiness and they give her their love.

When all the world was young, and nymphs and fauns dwelt in the forests, there was no nymph more lovely than the nymph named Echo. But, because of her beauty, she had been punished by the gods. Out of jealousy, the gods had taken away Echo's ability to speak. She was a slave to the tongues of others and could only repeat the last words others spoke. Despite her punishment, somehow Echo kept her merry heart—at least for a little while.

Narcissus was the beautiful son of a nymph and a river god. While hunting in the forest one day, Echo saw him pass by. Once she had seen him, she knew that she must gain his love or die. From that day on, she haunted him like his shadow, gliding from tree to tree, watching him from afar while he rested. So, she sought contentment by looking upon his face each day.

One day, Narcissus was separated from his companions in the chase. In the quiet woods, he heard the nymph's soft footfall on the rustling leaves.

"Who's here?" he called.

"*Here!*" answered Echo.

Narcissus, peering among the trees' long shadows and seeing no one, called "Come!"

And "*Come!*" called the glad voice of Echo, while the nymph, with fast-beating heart, felt that her day of happiness had indeed come.

"Why do you shun me?" then called Narcissus.

"*Why do you shun me?*" Echo repeated.

"Let us join one another," said the lad, and the simple words seemed turned into song when Echo said them over.

"*Let us join one another!*" she said, and she pushed aside the leaves of the trees and ran forward with outstretched arms to him.

With cold eyes and colder heart, the one she loved beheld her.

"Away!" he cried, shrinking back as if from something that he hated. "*Away!* I would rather die than that you should have me!"

"*Have me!*" cried Echo pitifully, but she pled in vain. Narcissus had no love to give her, and his scorn filled her with shame. After this, Echo hid her grief in the solitude of mountain cliffs and caves. For her, long nights and hopeless days told her that her love was all in vain. Over time, her body faded away, as an image on a photograph fades when the photograph has not been cared for. Only her voice was left to repeat and repeat.

Heart-whole and happy, Narcissus went on his way. Over time, other nymphs besides Echo also fell in love with him, but all in vain. He never returned their love. Eventually, the gods chose to punish Narcissus.

One day, Narcissus found a lonely pool in the woods. As he stooped down to drink, a face looked up through the crystal water, and a pair of beautiful eyes met his. He was sure that he was looking into the nymph of the pool. He was surprised and overjoyed at the sight of the most beautiful creature on Earth.

Round her head she had a circle of perfect curls, and her eyes were brown yet flecked with sunshine. When Narcissus smiled at her in rapture, her red lips also parted in a smile. He stretched out his arms toward her, and her arms stretched to him. Almost trembling in delight, he slowly stooped to kiss her. But when his mouth would have given itself to that other mouth—only the chilly water of the pool touched his lips, and the thing of his delight vanished away. In passionate disappointment, Narcissus waited for her to return; and as soon as the water of the pool grew still, once more he saw her exquisite face gazing up into his.

By day and by night, he haunted the forest pool. The moonbeams came straying down through the branches where he knelt by the pool. His face had become white, as if he'd been wounded. Mortally wounded he was, by a hopeless love for what was in truth but an image—an image in the water of his own face.

Echo and the other nymphs were avenged, yet they were filled with sorrow at the death of Narcissus. They filled the air with their lamentations, and most piteously did the voice of Echo repeat each mournful cry. Even the gods regretted their actions. And so, they turned Narcissus into a beautiful white flower, the flower that still bears his name and keeps his memory sweet.

13. Narcissus would BEST be described as a

    A. hero.

    B. villain.

    C. trickster.

    D. magic helper.

14. The author makes an analogy between Echo and a fading photograph to suggest that

    A. Echo can only be seen nowadays in old photographs.

    B. Echo was remembered by other people for a long time.

    C. Echo faded because she was not cared for by Narcissus.

    D. Echo lasted longer than most photographs.

15. What is the main idea of paragraph 4?

    A. Echo finds out that Narcissus doesn't love her.

    B. Narcissus likes to hunt every day in the forest.

    C. Echo falls in love with Narcissus as soon as she sees him.

    D. Nymphs and river gods should never be together.

16. Which of the following details from the passage BEST supports the idea that Narcissus found himself to be very beautiful?

    A. "He was sure that he was looking into the nymph of the pool. He was surprised and overjoyed at the sight of the most beautiful creature on Earth."

    B. "When all the world was young, and nymphs and fauns dwelt in the forests, there was no nymph more lovely than the nymph named Echo."

    C. "'Away!' he cried, shrinking back as if from something that he hated. '*Away!* I would rather die than that you should have me!'"

    D. "But, because of her beauty, she had been punished by the gods. Out of jealousy, the gods had taken away Echo's ability to speak."

17. What is the theme of the passage?

   A. Searching for love in the wrong places leads to sorrow.

   B. Go after what you want most in life and never give up.

   C. Honesty is always the best policy.

   D. Never compromise your standards.

18. Read this sentence from the passage.

   Despite her punishment, somehow Echo kept her merry heart—at least for a little while.

   Explain how the author uses this sentence to create a feeling of suspense. Use details from the passage to support your answer.

   _____

   _____

   _____

   _____

   _____

   _____

Read the passage and answer the questions that follow.

All or Nothing

The locusts buzzed loudly, but the players on the baseball field were silent. It was the top of the ninth inning of the championship game. The home team, the Vickstown Venoms, were beating the Hartsburg Hyenas by one run. The Venoms were on the field and their pitcher was only one out away from victory. If the next batter for the Hyenas struck out, then the Venoms would be champions for the first time in years. However, there was the Hyenas runner on third base to think about. If the next batter for the Hyenas got a big hit, there was a possibility the Venoms could lose the game.

Tension filled the air in the small stadium. The fans of the visiting team shouted: "We want a pitcher, not a belly itcher." It was a silly chant, but it made the Venoms even more nervous than they already were. The Venoms players were worriedly wringing their gloved hands and wiping the sweat from their brows. All eyes were on Marco—the star hitter for the Hyenas—as he strode up to the plate.

Rumors had circulated for the entire season that Marco was not an eighth-grader, but a high school player that the Hyenas had somehow managed to include on their team. He was at least a head taller than every other player on the field. As he warmed up, he swung the bat back and forth like he was attacking an army of imaginary enemies. He kicked the dirt around the plate until a cloud of dust rose up and was carried away by the wind.

The Hartsburg fans cheered. The Vickstown fans booed. But Marco only heard the cheers. He looked toward the visiting seats. The sun was so bright that he couldn't make out the faces of the fans. But he could imagine rows and rows of smiling faces—each and every fan looking at him, waving at him, clapping for him. He smiled and gripped the bat tightly.

The pitcher of the Vickstown Venoms pulled his arm back and let the ball rip through the air. A perfect curve ball! All the fans gasped. But Marco didn't swing.

"Why do I need to swing at that one?" he thought to himself. "That pitch wasn't good enough for the game-winning hit. Besides, there'll be at least two more pitches." Then he smiled up at his fans. While only a few fans clapped, to Marco's ears, these <u>sparse</u> gestures sounded like a roaring stadium. He turned once again and gripped his bat, ready for the next pitch.

The pitcher of the Vickstown Venoms grasped the ball once again. And for a second time, the ball sped through the air like an angry hornet. All the fans tensed in their seats. The Hartsburg fans were disappointed to see Marco resting the tip of his bat on the ground. He hadn't even bothered to hold up the bat. He was not aware of the real world around him. When he looked out into the stands, all he saw was his adoring fans smiling and waving. He believed that his fans knew the second pitch wasn't good enough for him to bother with.

The Venoms pitcher pulled back his arm and let the ball go once more. Marco gripped his bat and got ready. He could imagine exactly how he would smack the ball and send it into the stands. He could already picture himself holding the winning trophy, being carried on the shoulders of his teammates. He briefly fluttered his eyes and looked at the stands.

"Just one more time," he thought to himself, "I want to see my adoring fans and then I'll swing." As he glanced at the bleachers—*swoosh*—he heard a sound like a bird flying into a bush. It was the ball flying past his ear.

19. Read this sentence from the passage.

    While only a few fans clapped, to Marco's ears, these <u>sparse</u> gestures sounded like a roaring stadium.

    What is the meaning of the word <u>sparse</u> in this sentence?

    A. quiet

    B. pleasant

    C. few

    D. plentiful

20. Which event in the passage is part of the rising action?

    A. Marco hears "a sound like a bird flying" past his ear.

    B. The Vickstown Venoms wring their gloves.

    C. Marco pictures himself with a trophy.

    D. The Vickstown Venoms win the game.

21. Marco would BEST be described as a

    A. hero.

    B. villain.

    C. trickster.

    D. magic helper.

22. The author makes an analogy between the ball and a bird to suggest that

    A. the ball was moving into a tree.

    B. the ball was moving toward a bird.

    C. the sound of the ball was like the sound of a bird flying.

    D. a bird had flown past Marco, distracting him from the ball.

Use "Echo and Narcissus" and "All or Nothing" to answer questions 23–24.

23. The main character in each passage can BEST be described as

    A. overconfident.

    B. intelligent.

    C. compassionate.

    D. adventurous.

24. What is one theme that relates to both passages? Use details from the passages to support your answer.

    _____

    _____

    _____

    _____

    _____

    _____

Part 2: Language Arts

This passage contains mistakes. Read the passage and answer the questions that follow.

Can I Pay You with a Jedi?

(1) Do you love the *Star Wars* movies, such as *Return of the Jedi* and *The Phantom Menace*? (2) If so, you should consider taking a trip to Niue, a small island country located in the South Pacific.

(3) Fewer than two thousand people live in this island nation, which is about the number of people who live in a small town or small village in most countries. (4) Niue is so small, and you might not think anything particularly exciting could happen here. (5) But actually, this <u>diminutive</u> country has decided to do something very unusual; it's decided to design its own money in tribute to *Star Wars*.

(6) Up until now, the people living here have used New Zealand's currency, which makes sense since New Zealand is a nearby country. (7) But the people of Niue have decided it is time to have their own currency, and they came up with the idea for the *Star Wars* tribute. (8) Special coins were recently created to show characters from the world-renowned movie. (9) There are coins <u>depictting</u> Luke Skywalker, Darth Vader, Princess Leia, and others.

(10) Could you imagine fishing in your pocket for a quarter, and instead coming up with a coin with a green Yoda on its face? (11) Well, if you lived in or visited Niue, you'd be able to do just that.

(12) If you are interested in purchasing these coins, you can do so online. (13) But unless you live on Niue, these coins won't have any value as money. (14) The only place where they have any value as money or where you could in use possibly see them is on itself the island. (15) So, if you want to hear the jingle-jangle of Luke Skywalker and Darth Vader coins clinking onto the deli counter in exchange for a Slushee, you'd need to travel to Niue.

(16) For the most part, though, people are not expected to actually use these special, <u>exotick</u> coins to pay for things. (17) Most people are expected to acquire them for a collection. (18) This is, in part, due to the fact that the coins are made out of silver, which is a very <u>valuble</u> metal. (19) So, while one of these coins might be worth $2 and you could go into a store in Niue and buy $2 worth of candy with it, the coin is actually worth far, far more. (20) Some people are estimating that a single Niue coin could fetch as much as $100, simply because it's so unusual.

25. Read sentence 5.

> **But actually, this <u>diminutive</u> country has decided to do something very unusual; it's decided to design its own money in tribute to *Star Wars*.**

What reference source could you use to find a synonym for <u>diminutive</u>?

A. an encyclopedia

B. a thesaurus

C. a glossary

D. a newspaper

26. How should sentence 4 be edited?

A. Because Niue is so small, you might not think anything particularly exciting could happen here.

B. While Niue is so small, you might not think anything particularly exciting could happen here.

C. Although Niue is so small, you might not think anything particularly exciting could happen here.

D. Niue is so small, except you might not think anything particularly exciting could happen here.

27. Read sentence 9.

> **There are coins <u>depictting</u> Luke Skywalker, Darth Vader, Princess Leia, and others.**

What is the correct spelling of the word <u>depictting</u>?

A. deppictting

B. deppicting

C. depicting

D. dapicting

28. Read sentence 18.

> **This is, in part, due to the fact that the coins are made out of silver, which is a very <u>valuble</u> metal.**

What is the correct spelling of the word <u>valuble</u>?

A. valubel

B. valuabl

C. valueable

D. valuable

29. Read sentence 16.

    For the most part, though, people are not expected to actually use these special, <u>exotick</u> coins to pay for things.

What reference source would be BEST to use to determine the correct spelling of <u>exotick</u>?

    A. a dictionary

    B. an encyclopedia

    C. a magazine

    D. a thesaurus

30. Read sentence 14.

    The only place where they have any value as money or where you could in use possibly see them is on itself the island.

Revise this sentence on the lines below.

_____

_____

_____

_____

Part 3: Writing

Read the passage and respond to the prompt that follows.

The Secret Pleasures of Reginald
excerpted and adapted from **A Wodehouse Miscellany**
by P.G. Wodehouse

I found Reggie in the club one Saturday afternoon. He was reclining in a long chair, motionless, his eyes fixed glassily on the ceiling. He frowned a little when I spoke. "You don't seem to be doing anything," I said.

"It's not what I'm doing; it's what I am *not* doing that matters."

It sounded like an epigram, but epigrams are so little associated with Reggie that I ventured to ask what he meant.

He sighed. "Ah well," he said. "I suppose the sooner I tell you, the sooner you'll go. Do you know Bodfish?"

I shuddered. "Wilkinson Bodfish? I do."

"Have you ever spent a weekend at Bodfish's place in the country?"

I shuddered again. "I have."

"Well, I'm *not* spending the weekend at Bodfish's place in the country."

"I see you're not. But—"

"You don't understand. I do not mean that I am simply absent from Bodfish's place in the country. I mean that I am *deliberately* not spending the weekend there. When you interrupted me just now, I was not strolling down to Bodfish's garage, listening to his prattle about his new car."

I glanced around uneasily.

"Reggie, old man, you're—you're not—This hot weather—"

"I am perfectly well and in possession of all my faculties. Now tell me. Can you imagine anything more awful than to spend a weekend with Bodfish?"

On the spur of the moment, I could not.

"Can you imagine anything more delightful, then, than *not* spending a weekend with Bodfish? Well, that's what I'm doing now. Soon, when you have gone—if you have any other engagements, please don't let me keep you—I shall not go into the house and not listen to Mrs. Bodfish on the subject of young Willie Bodfish's premature intelligence."

I got his true meaning. "I see. You mean that you will be thanking your stars that you aren't with Bodfish."

"That is it, put crudely. But I go further. I don't indulge in a mere momentary self-congratulation, I do the thing thoroughly. If I were weekending at Bodfish's, I should have arrived there just half an hour ago. I therefore selected that moment for beginning not to weekend with Bodfish. I settled myself in this chair, and I did not have my back slapped at the station. A few minutes later, I was not whirling along the country roads, trying to balance the car with my legs and an elbow. Time passed, and I was not shaking hands with Mrs. Bodfish. I have just had the most relaxing half-hour, and shortly—when you have remembered an appointment—I shall go on having it. What I am really looking forward to is the happy time after dinner. I shall pass it in not playing bridge with Bodfish, Mrs. Bodfish, and a neighbor. Sunday morning is the best part of the whole weekend, though. That is when I shall most enjoy myself. Do you know a man named Pringle? Next Saturday, I am not going to stay with Pringle. I forget who is not to be my host the Saturday after that. I have so many engagements of this kind that I lose track of them."

"But, Reggie, this is genius. You have hit on the greatest idea of the age. You might extend this system of yours."

"I do. Some of the jolliest evenings I have spent have been not at the theatre."

"I have often wondered what it was that made you look so fit and happy."

"Yes. These little non-visits of mine pick me up and put life into me for the coming week. I get up on Monday morning feeling like a lion. The reason I selected Bodfish this week, though I had plans to visit a man named Stevenson who lives out in Connecticut, was that I felt rundown and needed a real rest. I shall be all right on Monday."

"And so shall I," I said, sinking into the chair beside him.

"You're not going to the country?" he asked regretfully.

"I am not. I, too, need a tonic. I shall join you at Bodfish's. I really feel a lot better already."

I closed my eyes and relaxed, and a great peace settled upon me.

Response to Literature Prompt

In the passage, the speaker says, "I shall join you at Bodfish's." Based on the passage, what does the speaker plan to do? Support your response with details from the passage.

Use the checklist below to help you do your best writing.

Does your response

❑ clearly introduce a claim?

❑ support the claim with relevant evidence from the passage?

❑ have a logical organization?

❑ demonstrate an understanding of the passage?

❑ use words, phrases, and clauses that show relationships among ideas?

❑ establish and maintain a formal style?

❑ consider purpose and audience?

❑ correctly use quotes from the passage?

Use the following pages to plan and write your response.

Planning Page

Benchmark Assessment 2

Part 1: Reading Comprehension

Read the passage and answer the questions that follow.

Unexpected Courage

When you think of courage, what comes to mind? Perhaps it's astronauts landing on the moon or firefighters saving people from a burning home. The life of artist Frida Kahlo is also a tale of unusual talent and remarkable courage.

Frida's life started out in a normal and expected way. She was born in Mexico on July 6, 1907. Her father, Guillermo, originally from Germany, had moved to Mexico, where he eventually met her mother, Matilde. Her father learned photography from his father-in-law and set up a photography business in Mexico. Frida lived with her parents in their home in Mexico.

One of the first serious challenges that Frida faced came at the age of six, when she was struck with polio. Nowadays, there is a polio vaccine. But back in the 1900s, polio was a terrifying worldwide epidemic, which particularly affected children and resulted in life-long disabilities. As a result of this disease, Frida's right foot became very thin and weak. Despite being so young, Frida worked regularly to exercise the muscles in her right foot. Even with her best efforts, she never fully regained the complete use of her right foot. So, she had to endure the teasing of other children.

Nonetheless, Frida had lofty aspirations. She decided she wanted to study to become a doctor, and she enrolled in the National Preparatory School. This was a very reputable school, and, at the time, only thirty-five girls were accepted to attend out of a total of two thousand students. Frida devoted herself to her studies, and, as a result of her hard work, she became fluent in Spanish, English, and German.

Unfortunately, tragedy would strike once again. During her senior year in 1925, with medical school just a few months away, Frida was involved in a major bus accident. The accident broke her pelvic bone and her spinal column, and it resulted in other injuries. Doctors had no idea whether or not Frida would live; and certainly, if she lived, they did not think she would ever walk again. Yet somehow, Frida survived.

For Frida, the accident changed everything. Suddenly, life was not about living and pursuing a medical career. Now, suddenly life was about surviving. She needed a series of painful operations, and she would be <u>bound</u> to her bed for a long time during her recovery.

Clearly, she could not attend medical school, yet somehow Frida took this tragedy and courageously turned it into inspiration. She asked for paints and canvasses. She then began to paint self-portraits from her bed, viewing herself by using a mirror. She hadn't had much experience with the arts before, but that didn't stop her. She painted and painted.

Eventually, Frida was able to walk again. But her ability to walk could never be taken for granted. Sometimes she could walk without support, sometimes she needed a cane or other support, and sometimes she would be bedridden for weeks or months.

In addition, because of the severity of the injuries to her spine, doctors required that she wear a corset off and on throughout the rest of her life. A corset is a stiff support, almost like a cast, that people wear around their waist and chest. For the rest of her lifetime, Frida would be required to wear painful corsets made out of steel as well as corsets made from plaster. The corsets could go from her hips to the top of her chest. They held her stiff so she could not bend or move. Another person might have lost hope and become completely unmotivated. But not Frida—she actually painted her plaster corsets. In addition, she painted self-portraits, in which she showed the world her broken bones and her body, stiff and immobilized in these corsets. So, in the end, she used the corsets as an inspiration.

Frida's paintings became known for the ways in which she uniquely represented her life. At the time, other painters depicted images of field workers or steel workers, or they created abstract and surreal images of objects such as melting clocks. Frida's paintings were unusual. She painted very realistic images of herself—her face, her corsets, her clothing, and the bed in which she was confined. But she blended this with more surreal imagery—such as banners being held aloft by doves, walking skeletons, and her chest opened to show her heart. She blended the real and surreal to show her thoughts, feelings, and sensations to the world. From looking at a series of her paintings, a viewer would be able to see the secrets of her life: her injuries, her love life, and the problems she had with family.

Over the course of her life, Frida suffered through more than thirty surgeries. Despite her injuries, she traveled the world to show her paintings. Frida Kahlo passed away in 1954 at the age of forty-seven. Despite her physical suffering, she persevered and created a wealth of paintings that are still admired and respected around the world. In total, Frida painted well over a hundred paintings, of which more than fifty were self-portraits. As she said herself, she painted so many self-portraits "because I am so often alone … because I am the subject I know best."

The Two Fridas by Frida Kahlo

1. Which of the following details from the passage BEST supports the conclusion that Frida Kahlo is a well-respected artist?

   A. "Frida devoted herself to her studies, and, as a result of her hard work, she became fluent in Spanish, English, and German."

   B. "Despite her physical suffering, she persevered and created a wealth of paintings that are still admired and respected around the world."

   C. "She hadn't had much experience with the arts before, but that didn't stop her."

   D. "But not Frida—she actually painted her plaster corsets."

2. Read this sentence from the passage.

   One of the first serious challenges that Frida faced came at the age of six, when she was struck with polio.

   The statement that Frida was "struck with polio" means that

   A. Frida got the disease by being hit by someone.

   B. the disease happened to children who were in accidents.

   C. the disease made Frida fall down instantaneously.

   D. the disease quickly caused serious health problems.

3. What is the BEST summary of the passage?

   A. Frida Kahlo endured many challenges in her life, such as problems with polio, a serious bus accident, and multiple surgeries.

   B. Frida Kahlo's paintings combine realistic elements as well as surrealistic elements to form unique and meaningful artwork.

   C. Despite Frida Kahlo's serious health problems, she managed to survive courageously and became a world-renowned painter.

   D. Unlike other artists at the time, Frida Kahlo revealed the details of her private life in her paintings, such as her surgeries and relationship problems.

4. Read this sentence from the passage.

   She needed a series of painful operations, and she would be bound to her bed for a long time during her recovery.

   What is the meaning of the word bound in this sentence?

   A. restricted

   B. tied

   C. jumping

   D. forbidden

5. Read these sentences from the passage.

> **Another person might have lost hope and become completely unmotivated. But not Frida—she actually painted her plaster corsets.**

The author included these sentences to

A. imply that Frida recovered from her injuries easily.

B. reveal a feeling of respect and admiration for Frida.

C. explain why readers should pity Frida.

D. suggest that Frida's injuries were unimportant.

6. What is the main idea of the passage? Use details from the passage to support your answer.

_____

_____

_____

_____

_____

_____

_____

_____

Read the passage and answer the questions that follow.

Space Garden

Looking out the window, Jorge thought, "I am the luckiest guy on Earth to be able to see what I am seeing." Then he chuckled to himself. "Of course, I'm not *on* Earth. If I were, I wouldn't have this view." Again, he looked out the window of the International Space Station and saw his home planet drifting slowly by, 220 miles away.

There was time for daydreaming on the space station, but there was also plenty of work to do. Now Jorge had to tend to his mission's main experiment: the space garden, as he and the other two crewmembers called it.

He floated toward the Laboratory Module, where the experimental garden was growing. Floating around the space station in zero gravity was a fun part of the job.

When Jorge reached the Laboratory Module, Pilot Steve Wong and Commander Elya Gordeeva were already checking out one of the experiments.

"Jorge, what are you up to?" asked Elya.

"I have to go tend to my plants," he responded.

Actually, most of the work had been done back on Earth. Scientists had developed the growth chamber, a completely enclosed tray where the temperature, humidity, light, and delivery of water and nutrients to the plants were controlled by a computer. The scientists had planted seeds in a rooting material and had attached the seed tray to the growth chamber. All that Jorge had to do was to check the plants now and then and report what he saw to the lab.

Jorge removed the growth chamber from the rack and peered at it. He could see small green shoots. It looked like most of the seeds had germinated. Without realizing what he was doing, Jorge began to talk to the plants. As if he had found a small lost child, Jorge introduced himself and offered encouraging words.

"What did you say, Jorge?" Steve asked as he floated over.

"I'm not talking to you, Steve. Just giving the Arabidopsis some encouragement."

"Who?"

"Arabidopsis! The plants we're growing. They're related to cabbages and radishes. The scientists say that if we can grow plants that produce seeds in microgravity, future space missions could grow their own fresh vegetables."

"Uh-huh," nodded Steve. "And did the scientists tell you to talk to the plants?"

"Well, not exactly. My grandma read this book once. It said that if you talk to your houseplants, they'll grow better. So I thought it couldn't hurt to give the Arabidopsis a few friendly words."

"Elya," Steve called. "This guy is talking to the plants. Do you think we should notify the doctor?"

Elya laughed. "I don't think there's anything wrong with Jorge. But if those plants get too big, the lab's not going to be happy. They specifically chose a plant species that wouldn't grow too large."

"Laugh all you want," grinned Jorge. "But I'm planning to take some prize-winning Arabidopsis back to Earth. A few years from now, when you're orbiting Mars and eating fresh greens, you just remember it was Jorge Mendes who encouraged their great-grandmother to produce good seeds."

That night, Jorge was listening to music through his headphones. Elya was e-mailing her family in Russia. Steve floated up to her when Jorge wasn't looking.

"Elya, I've got a great idea for a trick to play on Jorge. We'll make an audio recording of me talking to him as if I'm one of the plants. Then we'll hide the recorder near the plants. The next time he works there, one of us will sneak over and push the PLAY button."

"What will you say in the recording?" asked Elya.

"Oh, I'll tell him how glad all of us plants are that he is taking such good care of us."

"You think he will believe that?" asked Elya.

"Not really, but it'll be a good laugh," chuckled Steve.

"OK, let's do it!" they both agreed.

A few weeks later, Jorge had to refill the nutrient container for the plant chamber. As he worked, he muttered to the plants. Steve floated over.

Suddenly, Jorge heard a low voice. But Steve's lips weren't moving.

"Did you hear that?" Jorge asked.

"I didn't hear anything," Steve replied. "Did you hear anything, Elya?"

"Nyet," she answered.

Jorge tried his best to control the grin that was breaking out on his face. "I could swear the plants were talking back to me. They said they're glad I'm taking care of them."

"Really?" asked Steve, trying to hide his own grin.

"Yes," Jorge laughed. "Funny thing is, I talk to them in Spanish, but they're answering in English."

With that, the astronauts had a good laugh as they celebrated the progress of their prized cargo.

7. What is the point of view of the passage?

   A. first person

   B. second person

   C. third person, limited

   D. third person, omniscient

8. What is the theme of the passage?

   A. People are often frightened of things they don't understand.

   B. Listen to your elders who have wisdom and experience.

   C. Finding ways to have fun on the job can make work more enjoyable.

   D. It can be boring to spend a lot of time working with people you do not know well.

9. Which event in the passage is part of the climax?

   A. Steve plays a recording of the "plants" talking.

   B. Jorge looks out the window at Earth.

   C. Elya spends time e-mailing her family in Russia.

   D. Jorge says encouraging things to the plants.

10. Jorge would BEST be described as a

   A. hero.

   B. villain.

   C. trickster.

   D. magic helper.

11. The author makes an analogy between the seedlings and small lost children to suggest that

   A. the seedlings are confused about being in space.

   B. Jorge wants to bring the seedlings back to Earth.

   C. the seedlings need to be treated with kindness.

   D. the seedlings will take a long time to grow to adult plants.

12. Which word BEST describes Jorge and why? Use details from the passage to support your answer.

   _____

   _____

   _____

   _____

   _____

   _____

Read the passage and answer the questions that follow.

A Fight for Rights

The United States was founded in 1776 on the principles of independence, freedom, and rights. Yet, it took many years plus the hard work and diligence of thousands of people before laws were put in place in the United States to protect the civil rights of everyone.

The Emancipation Proclamation

The original goal of the Civil War was to restore the Union—to keep North and South joined together. It was not originally a war about the issue of slavery. But some advisors to President Abraham Lincoln suggested that if he freed the slaves, it would weaken the Confederacy. The Confederate Army relied on slave labor to supply much of the food and materials soldiers needed. In 1863, Lincoln signed the Emancipation Proclamation, which stated that "all persons held as slaves" in areas under Confederate control were to be "forever free." It did not, however, free enslaved African Americans in Union states or in Southern cities already controlled by the Union, such as New Orleans.

Because the Confederate states were not under Union rule at the time, the Emancipation Proclamation did not actually free any slaves. But the Proclamation did affect the purpose of the war. After the war, Congress passed three important <u>amendments</u> to the Constitution. In 1865, the Thirteenth Amendment abolished slavery. The Fourteenth Amendment in 1868 granted citizenship and equal protection under the law to former slaves and to any other person born or naturalized in the United States. In 1870, the Fifteenth Amendment guaranteed every male citizen the right to vote. These three amendments became known as the Civil War Amendments.

The Process of Amending the Constitution

The process of passing an amendment to the Constitution is not easy. The Founding Fathers did not want the Constitution to be changed frequently; they wanted it to endure. But they always wanted to insure that it could be changed under very important circumstances. Here are the steps needed to pass an amendment to the Constitution.

Step 1: First, the amendment must be proposed. This can happen when:
  • EITHER two-thirds of the state legislatures agree to propose the amendment
  • OR two-thirds of both the Senate and the House of Representatives agree to propose the amendment.

Step 2: Once the amendment is proposed, it is sent to the Office of the Federal Register, where it is printed.

Step 3: The amendment is submitted to every state governor in the United States. Each governor must submit the amendment to his or her state legislature.

Step 4: If three-fourths of the state legislatures approve the amendment, then it can be added to the United States Constitution.

Step 5: The Office of the Federal Register prints the amendment on a certificate.

Step 6: The president signs the certificate.

The Loss of Freedom

After the Civil War, African American men had the right to register to vote and run for public office. Fear of this growing political power caused hate groups, such as the Ku Klux Klan, to organize throughout the South. Wearing white robes and hoods, Klansmen terrorized or murdered members of minority groups, including African American men who dared to vote.

Southern politicians looked for ways to get around the Fifteenth Amendment. They created laws that required voters to be able to read, relying on the fact that many African American men were uneducated. Politicians imposed poll taxes, which required voters to pay in order to register to vote. This action would prevent poor former slaves from being able to vote. In some states, special "grandfather clauses" allowed a man to vote only if his father or grandfather had been a registered voter on January 1, 1867. Such laws kept African American men from voting.

Separate but Equal

After 1877, the South passed "Jim Crow" laws. These laws segregated African Americans from white people in public places. Jim Crow laws forced African Americans to eat in separate restaurants, travel in separate railway cars, attend separate schools and theaters, be treated in separate hospitals, and even be buried in separate cemeteries.

In 1896, an African American challenged the Jim Crow laws in a lawsuit called *Plessy v. Ferguson.* The state of Louisiana upheld the conviction of an African American man named Homer Plessy for riding in a whites-only railway car. Plessy took his case to the Supreme Court. The justices ruled that state governments could segregate people of different races as long as the separate facilities were equal. The basis for this ruling was called the "separate but equal" doctrine.

Separate and Unequal

Many African Americans began to demand justice. In 1909, after a white mob started a race riot in Springfield, Illinois, a group of African American and white citizens organized the National Association for the Advancement of Colored People (NAACP) to help fight for civil rights.

One of the many important cases that the NAACP was involved in happened in 1954. Thirteen African American parents in Topeka, Kansas, tried to enroll their children in all-white public schools. When the schools refused, the NAACP helped the parents file a lawsuit. In a case called *Brown v. Board of Education,* the lawsuit claimed that the separate but equal doctrine denied children an equal education.

On May 17, 1954, the Supreme Court ruled unanimously that *Plessy v. Ferguson*'s separate but equal doctrine was unconstitutional. Chief Justice Warren stated that "segregated schools are not equal and cannot be made equal and hence they [African American children] are deprived [denied] of the equal protection of the laws." The next year, the Supreme Court ordered an end to segregated schools.

In the period from 1953 to 1968, African Americans made more advances in equal rights than at any time since the Civil War. The Civil Rights Acts of 1957 and 1960 aimed to safeguard voting rights. The Twenty-Fourth Amendment, passed in 1964, outlawed discriminatory voting laws. The Civil Rights Act of 1964 included protections for equal opportunity in employment and housing. But many Southern whites still believed in segregation.

An Important Leader

In 1955, the arrest of Rosa Parks for refusing to give up her seat on a bus to a white man gave national attention to a new civil rights leader. A young Baptist minister, Dr. Martin Luther King Jr., helped lead a boycott of buses in Montgomery, Alabama. The boycott was successful, and, a year later, the Supreme Court ruled that Alabama's segregation laws for public transportation were unconstitutional.

In 1965, civil rights workers in Selma, Alabama, were threatened and arrested while trying to register African American voters. Dr. King organized 40,000 people in a nonviolent protest and marched from Selma to Montgomery, the state capital. Because of the Selma March and other nonviolent boycotts, Congress finally passed the Voting Rights Act of 1965. This act eliminated all tests for people registering to vote and guaranteed federal protection to all voters. President Lyndon Johnson signed the Voting Rights Act as well as the Civil Rights Act of 1968, which banned discrimination in the sale and rental of housing. One hundred years after the Constitution abolished slavery, Congress fulfilled the promises of the Civil War Amendments.

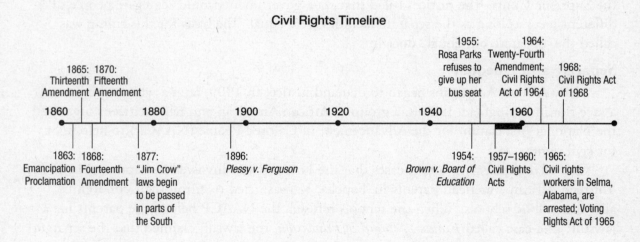

Civil Rights Timeline

13. What happens after three-fourths of the state legislatures approve an amendment?

   A. Two-thirds of both the Senate and House of Representatives must agree to the amendment.

   B. The Office of the Federal Register prints the amendment on a certificate.

   C. The governor of each state must submit the amendment to his or her state legislature.

   D. Two-thirds of the state legislatures must propose the amendment to the Congress.

14. Which of the following is an opinion from the passage?

   A. "In 1865, the Thirteenth Amendment abolished slavery."

   B. "Such laws kept African American men from voting."

   C. "In 1896, an African American challenged the Jim Crow laws in a lawsuit called *Plessy v. Ferguson*."

   D. "After the war, Congress passed three important amendments to the Constitution."

15. Which of the following resulted from the passing of the Voting Rights Act of 1965?

   A. The voting rights of African Americans were federally protected.

   B. Slaves in Confederate states became free.

   C. State governments were allowed to keep "separate but equal" laws in place.

   D. Buses in Alabama were no longer allowed to be segregated.

16. Read this sentence from the passage.

   Chief Justice Warren stated that "segregated schools are not equal and cannot be made equal and hence they [African American children] are deprived [denied] of the equal protection of the laws."

   Which of the following BEST explains the type of source that this sentence represents?

   A. This is a primary source because it tells what Chief Justice Warren actually said.

   B. This is a primary source because it is about a person and an event that happened many years ago.

   C. This is a secondary source because it expresses a person's opinion about an event.

   D. This is a secondary source because it is a recollection that someone has of what Chief Justice Warren said.

17. According to the time line, which event happened BEFORE the ratification of the Twenty-Fourth Amendment?

A. Civil rights workers in Selma, Alabama, were arrested.

B. The Civil Rights Act of 1968 was passed.

C. Rosa Parks refused to give up her bus seat.

D. The Voting Rights Act of 1965 was passed.

18. Throughout the passage, the term <u>amendment</u> is used. Write your own definition of the term <u>amendment</u> using details from the passage.

_____

_____

_____

_____

Read the passage and answer the questions that follow.

excerpted from

Radio and Television Report to the American People on Civil Rights
by President John F. Kennedy
speech given at the White House on June 11, 1963

Good evening, my fellow citizens:

. . . Today we are committed to a worldwide struggle to promote and protect the rights of all who wish to be free. And when Americans are sent to Viet-Nam or West Berlin, we do not ask for whites only. It ought to be possible, therefore, for American students of any color to attend any public institution they select without having to be backed up by troops.

It ought to be possible for American consumers of any color to receive equal service in places of public <u>accommodation</u>, such as hotels and restaurants and theaters and retail stores, without being forced to resort to demonstrations in the street, and it ought to be possible for American citizens of any color to register to vote in a free election without interference or fear of reprisal.

It ought to be possible, in short, for every American to enjoy the privileges of being American without regard to his race or his color. In short, every American ought to have the right to be treated as he would wish to be treated, as one would wish his children to be treated. But this is not the case. . . .

President Kennedy addresses the
nation on civil rights. (June 11, 1963)

The heart of the question is whether all Americans are to be afforded equal rights and equal opportunities, whether we are going to treat our fellow Americans as we want to be treated. If an American, because his skin is dark, cannot eat lunch in a restaurant open to the public, if he cannot send his children to the best public school available, if he cannot vote for the public officials who will represent him, if, in short, he cannot enjoy the full and free life which all of us want, then who among us would be content to have the color of his skin changed and stand in his place? Who among us would then be content with the counsels of patience and delay?

One hundred years of delay have passed since President Lincoln freed the slaves, yet their heirs, their grandsons, are not fully free. They are not yet freed from the bonds of injustice. They are not yet freed from social and economic oppression. And this Nation, for all its hopes and all its boasts, will not be fully free until all its citizens are free. . . .

Now the time has come for this Nation to fulfill its promise. The events in Birmingham and elsewhere have so increased the cries for equality that no city or State or legislative body can prudently choose to ignore them.

The fires of frustration and discord are burning in every city, North and South, where legal remedies are not at hand. Redress is sought in the streets, in demonstrations, parades, and protests which create tensions and threaten violence and threaten lives.

We face, therefore, a moral crisis as a country and as a people. It cannot be met by repressive police action. It cannot be left to increased demonstrations in the streets. It cannot be quieted by token moves or talk. It is time to act in the Congress, in your State and local legislative body and, above all, in all of our daily lives…

Those who do nothing are inviting shame as well as violence. Those who act boldly are recognizing right as well as reality. . . .

I am, therefore, asking the Congress to enact legislation giving all Americans the right to be served in facilities which are open to the public—hotels, restaurants, theaters, retail stores, and similar establishments.

This seems to me to be an elementary right. Its denial is an arbitrary indignity that no American in 1963 should have to endure, but many do.

I have recently met with scores of business leaders urging them to take voluntary action to end this discrimination and I have been encouraged by their response, and in the last two weeks over seventy-five cities have seen progress made in desegregating these kinds of facilities. But many are unwilling to act alone, and for this reason, nationwide legislation is needed if we are to move this problem from the streets to the courts…

Other features will also be requested, including greater protection for the right to vote. But legislation, I repeat, cannot solve this problem alone. It must be solved in the homes of every American in every community across our country.

In this respect I want to pay tribute to those citizens North and South who have been working in their communities to make life better for all. They are acting not out of a sense of legal duty but out of a sense of human decency.

We cannot say to 10 percent of the population that you can't have that right; that your children cannot have the chance to develop whatever talents they have; that the only way that they are going to get their rights is to go into the streets and demonstrate. I think we owe them and we owe ourselves a better country than that.

Therefore, I am asking for your help in making it easier for us to move ahead and to provide the kind of equality of treatment which we would want ourselves; to give a chance for every child to be educated to the limit of his talents...

This is what we are talking about and this is a matter which concerns this country and what it stands for, and in meeting it I ask the support of all our citizens.

Thank you very much.

19. Which term from the passage would MOST LIKELY be found in the glossary of a social studies textbook?

A. frustration

B. legislation

C. nationwide

D. decency

20. Which of the following is a fact from the passage?

A. "I think we owe them and we owe ourselves a better country than that."

B. "It ought to be possible for American citizens of any color to register to vote in a free election. . . ."

C. "I have recently met with scores of business leaders urging them to take voluntary action. . . ."

D. "Now the time has come for this Nation to fulfill its promise."

21. Which of the following BEST explains why this passage is an example of a primary source?

A. It is a speech.

B. It is from 1963.

C. It tells about American history.

D. It describes Kennedy's opinions.

22. Read the dictionary entry below for the word accommodation.

accommodation *n.* **1.** an adjustment **2.** a place that offers food, lodging, or other services **3.** willingness to help **4.** a loan

Which definition represents the meaning of accommodation as it is used in paragraph 2?

A. definition 1

B. definition 2

C. definition 3

D. definition 4

Use "A Fight for Rights" and President Kennedy's civil rights speech to answer questions 23–24.

23. Look at this diagram of information from the passages.

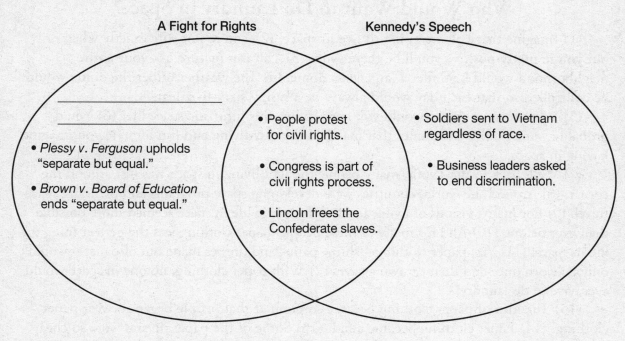

Which detail belongs on the blank lines?

A. More than seventy-five cities make progress toward desegregation.

B. Role of Dr. Martin Luther King Jr. is important.

C. Support of all citizens is asked for.

D. Soldiers of all colors are sent to West Berlin.

24. Why did the authors MOST LIKELY write each passage? Use details from the passages to support your answer.

_____

_____

_____

_____

_____

_____

Read the passage and answer the questions that follow.

Who Would Want to Do Laundry in Space?

(1) Imagine that you are going to live in space. (2) You're not sure exactly when, but you're pretty <u>positive</u> you'll be there soon. (3) You can picture it—your entire neighborhood would be under a large glass dome. (4) The weather under the dome would be controlled so that each day would always be a sunny sixty-five degrees!

(5) What sorts of things would you need to live this futuristic space life? (6) You'd probably want clothes and games that matched the easy-living and fun lifestyle you imagine having in space.

(7) Well, back in the 1960s, many people thought living in space was just around the corner. (8) Around the world, countries were developing space programs and planning space travel. (9) For many, visions of living an ideal, futuristic life in space seemed more possible than ever before. (10) And for many of these people, paper clothing was the perfect thing for life in space! (11) Yes, paper clothing—shirts, pants, and dresses made out of paper—would only be worn once and then thrown away. (12) With paper clothing, no one in space would ever have to do laundry!

(13) The idea of paper clothing became so popular that people began to wear paper clothing. (14) Paper clothing became a fad. (15) Some of the paper dresses were so cheap that people could pick one up for just about a dollar! (16) Many companies got into the disposable paper clothing business. (17) Some paper dress companies made other paper products. (18) They might even have made toilet paper. (19) Back then, people who bought a paper dress could receive a coupon for toilet paper! (20) Some designers even came up with high-end paper clothing, such as ball gowns and hand-painted dresses made out of paper.

(21) Needless to say, the paper dress fad eventually faded, as most fads do. (22) Paper clothing was replaced by the next hip fads, such as bell-bottoms and embroidered peasant blouses. (23) Also, many people were concerned about the environment, as <u>disposable</u> clothing produced a lot of unnecessary waste.

(24) We do not yet live on the moon or in space stations <u>orbiting</u> strange alien planets. (25) The thought of living in space may seem like a dream, but paper clothing still exists. (26) You may have been asked to wear a paper gown during a doctor's appointment. (27) And paper clothing is provided to patients in hospitals. (28) Paper clothing may not be as popular as people once expected, but it has endured.

25. What is the BEST way to combine sentences 17 and 18?

A. Some paper dress companies made other paper products, such as toilet paper.

B. Some paper dress companies made other paper products, and some paper dress companies might even have made toilet paper.

C. Some paper dress companies made other paper products, including paper products like toilet paper.

D. Some paper dress companies made other paper products and toilet paper.

26. Read sentence 24.

We do not yet live on the moon or in space stations orbiting strange alien planets.

What is the MOST LIKELY reason that the author uses the word orbiting?

A. to tell readers how space stations move nowadays

B. to tell readers how space stations used to move

C. to describe how space stations could move

D. to describe the space stations of aliens

27. Read sentence 2.

You're not sure exactly when, but you're pretty positive you'll be there soon.

Based on the context clues, what is the meaning of positive?

A. clearly stated

B. the results of a test

C. electrically charged

D. very sure of something

28. Reread sentence 10.

And for many of these people, paper clothing was the perfect thing for life in space!

In this sentence, the author MOST LIKELY means that

A. people were perfect.

B. paper clothing was perfect.

C. life in space was perfect.

D. things in space were perfect.

29. Reread sentence 1.

Imagine that you are going to live in space.

The author uses the phrase "to live" to describe an action that

A. happened a long time ago.

B. just happened.

C. is happening right now.

D. could happen in the future.

30. Read sentence 23.

Also, many people were concerned about the environment, as <u>disposable</u> clothing produced a lot of unnecessary waste.

What is the meaning of the word <u>disposable</u>? Use context clues from the passage to support your answer.

_____

_____

_____

_____

_____

_____

Part 3: Writing

Personal Narrative Prompt

Write a narrative about the first time you heard a song that later became one of your favorite songs. Be sure to describe where you were when you heard it, what you were doing, who you were with, and how hearing the song the first time made you feel.

Use the checklist below to help you do your best writing.

Does your narrative

❏ have an engaging introduction?

❏ establish a background and point of view?

❏ organize an event sequence that unfolds naturally and logically?

❏ consider purpose and audience?

❏ use narrative techniques to develop experiences, events, and characters?

❏ use a variety of transitions to convey sequence and show relationships between ideas?

❏ use precise and descriptive language?

❏ have a thoughtful conclusion?

Use the following pages to plan and write your response.

Planning Page

Benchmark Assessment

3

Part 1: Reading Comprehension

Read the passage and answer the questions that follow.

excerpted and adapted from

The Boy Comes Home: A Comedy in One Act
by A.A. Milne

CAST OF CHARACTERS

Uncle James
Aunt Emily
Philip
Mary, the maid
Mrs. Higgins, the cook

(*A room in Uncle James's house, the day after the end of World War I. The room is furnished in heavy mid-Victorian style; this particular morning room is perhaps solider and more respectable even than the others, from the heavy table in the middle of it to the heavy engravings on the walls.*)

(*Philip comes from the hall and goes into the dining room. Apparently he finds nothing there, for he returns to the morning room, looks about him for a moment and then rings the bell. It is ten o'clock, and he wants his breakfast.*)

MARY: Did you ring, Master Philip?

PHILIP: (*absently*) Yes, I want some breakfast, please, Mary.

MARY: (*coldly*) Breakfast has been cleared away an hour ago.

PHILIP: (*looking down at his paper*) Exactly. That's why I rang. You can boil me a couple of eggs or something. And coffee, not tea.

MARY: I'm sure I don't know what Mrs. Higgins will say. She's not used to being put about like this.

PHILIP: Do you think she'll say something?

MARY: I don't know *what* she'll say.

PHILIP: You needn't tell me, you know, if you don't want to. Anyway, I don't suppose it will shock me. One gets used to it in the army. (*He smiles pleasantly at her.*)

MARY: Well, I'll do what I can, sir. But breakfast at eight sharp is the master's rule, just as it used to be before you went away to the war.

PHILIP: (*more curtly*) Two eggs, and if there's a ham, bring that along, too.

MARY: (*doubtfully, as she prepares to go*) Well, I'm sure I don't know what Mrs. Higgins will say.

(*Exit Mary. As she goes out, she makes way for Aunt Emily to come in, a kind-hearted mid-Victorian lady.*)

EMILY: There you are, Philip! Good morning, dear. Did you sleep well?

PHILIP: Rather splendidly, thanks, Aunt Emily. How are you? (*He kisses her.*)

EMILY: And did you have a good breakfast? Naughty boy to be late for it. I always thought they had to get up so early in the army.

PHILIP: They do. That's why they're so late when they get out of the army.

EMILY: Dear me! I should have thought a habit of four years would have stayed with you.

PHILIP: Every morning for four years, as I've shot out of bed, I've said to myself, "Wait! A time will come." (*smiling*) That doesn't really give a habit a chance.

EMILY: Well, I daresay you wanted to sleep. I was so afraid that a really cozy bed would keep you awake after all those years in the trenches.

(*Enter Mary.*)

MARY: Mrs. Higgins wishes to speak to you, ma'am. (*She looks at Philip.*)

PHILIP: (*firmly to Mary*) Tell Mrs. Higgins to come here. (*Mary hesitates and looks at her mistress.*) At once, please. (*Exit Mary.*)

EMILY: (*upset*) Philip, dear, I don't know what Mrs. Higgins will say—

PHILIP: No; nobody seems to. I thought we might really find out for once.

EMILY: (*going toward the door*) Perhaps I'd better go—

PHILIP: (*putting his arm round her waist*) Oh no, you mustn't. You see, she really wants to see *me*.

EMILY: *You?*

PHILIP: Yes, I ordered breakfast five minutes ago.

EMILY: Philip! My poor boy! Why didn't you tell me? I daresay I could have got it for you. (*An extremely angry voice is heard, and Mrs. Higgins, stout and aggressive, comes in.*)

MRS. HIGGINS: (*crossly*) You sent for me, ma'am?

EMILY: (*nervously*) Yes—er—I think if you—perhaps—

PHILIP: (*calmly*) *I* sent for you, Mrs. Higgins. I want some breakfast. Didn't Mary tell you?

MRS. HIGGINS: Breakfast is at eight o'clock. It always has been as long as I've been in this house, and always will be until I get further orders.

PHILIP: Well, you've just got further orders. Two eggs, and if there's a ham—

MRS. HIGGINS: Orders? From whom in this house do I take orders, may I ask?

PHILIP: In this case from me.

MRS. HIGGINS: (*playing her trump card*) In that case, ma'am, I wish to give a month's notice from today. Inclusive.

PHILIP: (*quickly, before his aunt can say anything*) Certainly. In fact, you'd probably prefer it if my aunt gave *you* notice, and then you could go at once. We can easily arrange that. (*to Aunt Emily as he takes out a fountain pen and checkbook*) What do you pay her?

EMILY: (*faintly*) Forty-five pounds.

PHILIP: (*writes a check on his knee and tears it out*) Here you are.

MRS. HIGGINS: (*taken aback*) What's this?

PHILIP: Your wages instead of notice. Now you can go at once.

MRS. HIGGINS: Who said anything about going?

PHILIP: (*surprised*) *You* did.

MRS. HIGGINS: If it's only a bit of breakfast, I don't say but what I mightn't get it, if I'm asked decent.

PHILIP: (*putting back the check*) Then let me say again, "Two eggs, ham, and coffee."

MRS. HIGGINS: Well, I—well—well! (*She exits, speechless.*)

PHILIP: (*surprised*) Is that all she ever says? It isn't much to worry about.

EMILY: Philip, how could you! I should have been terrified.

PHILIP: Well, you see, I've done your job for two years out there.

EMILY: What job?

PHILIP: Officer in charge of the Mess Hall. I think I'll go and see about that ham.

(*He smiles at her and goes out into the dining room.*)

1. What does breakfast symbolize in this passage?

   A. wealth

   B. forgiveness

   C. youth

   D. power

2. What is the genre of this passage?

   A. a poem

   B. a play

   C. a short story

   D. an autobiography

3. Read these sentences from the passage.

   MARY: I'm sure I don't know what Mrs. Higgins will say. She's not used to being put about like this.

   The author uses the phrase "I don't know what Mrs. Higgins will say" to suggest that

   A. Mrs. Higgins doesn't normally speak.

   B. Mary thinks Mrs. Higgins will be angry.

   C. Mary doesn't like speaking with Mrs. Higgins.

   D. Mrs. Higgins isn't used to being asked questions.

4. Read these sentences from the passage.

   MRS. HIGGINS: (*playing her trump card*) In that case, ma'am, I wish to give a month's notice from today. Inclusive.

   The author uses the phrase "trump card" to suggest that Mrs. Higgins

   A. has written out her notice on a piece of paper.

   B. is holding mail in her hands.

   C. wants to hand Philip a playing card.

   D. is saying something that she thinks will win the argument.

5. Which of the following BEST describes the mood of this passage?

   A. joyful

   B. tense

   C. scary

   D. grateful

6. In the play, Philip writes a check to pay Mrs. Higgins her wages. Is this an example of dramatic irony? Why or why not? Use details from the passage to support your answer.

   _____

   _____

   _____

   _____

   _____

   _____

Read the passage and answer the questions that follow.

Shaping the News

People have always been hungry for news, wanting more and more whether it is good or bad. Before the printing press and computers, Native Americans used smoke signals or drum beats to send news. Today, television, newspapers, radio, and the Internet satisfy an even bigger appetite for news. At any time of day, people can read about an election or a sports event, listen to celebrity gossip, or learn about space travel and new technologies. With so much information available, readers and viewers need to be selective about *what* they read and hear. It is also important to understand the difference between fact and opinion and to be able to detect bias.

For most of our nation's history, newspapers have delivered the news. Some newspapers started as small-town journals that sold for a penny. Others were started in cities that grew in size as the population grew. All of these newspapers have made a difference in people's lives. Freedom of the press has made this possible. The First Amendment guarantees this freedom, but there is no guarantee that what people read or listen to will be truthful. Bias in the media does exist. Most reporters try not to show bias. They attempt to give their readers or viewers fair, <u>objective</u> information. It is their job to present all sides of a story, helping readers to decide for themselves what's true and what's not.

Promoting the West

This commitment to fairness has not always been a part of journalism in America. Newspapers in the colonial era and in the 1800s carried many stories that reported only one side of an issue or promoted the ideas of one political party. They clearly tried to influence people's opinions or emotions. This was evident during the settlement of the West. As towns sprang up near rivers and railroads, so did newspapers. Printers either traveled with the settlers or followed them and would quickly start a newspaper. Such newspapers bragged about their town's bright future and exaggerated what the town had to offer. Because the success of these newspapers depended on the growth of population in the towns, the printers needed to attract more settlers. They even called these towns "cities" to exaggerate their size.

New York newspaperman Horace Greeley, who visited Kansas in 1859, wrote, "It takes three log houses to make a city in Kansas, but they begin calling it a city so soon as they have staked out the lots." If these new "cities" failed to survive, the printers just moved on.

The discovery of gold also gave birth to new towns. Because printers knew that their success depended on the number of people buying their newspapers, they boasted in their newspapers that the nearby gold strike was the richest ever found, attracting more miners. If miners streamed into the town and did not find gold, they told others that the boom was a hoax. It would not take long for the printers to move on to the next mining camp and a new population of readers.

New Journalism Style

In 1883, a new style of journalism became popular. Joseph Pulitzer, who owned the *New York World,* wanted to crusade for reforms that helped the working class. His newspapers carried news that touched the emotions of readers. Pulitzer said that the *World* "should always be devoted to the public welfare, be drastically independent, and never afraid to attack wrong." His aggressive style of investigative reporting changed the standards for newspapers worldwide.

Pulitzer's main rival was William Randolph Hearst, owner of the *New York Journal.* Pulitzer and Hearst both wanted to sell the most newspapers and to be the first with the news. Hearst urged his reporters to sensationalize their stories. The *Journal* and the *World* ran headlines and pictures that shocked or scared readers. Pages were filled with rumors and scandals. To boost sales of his newspaper, Pulitzer started to print Sunday comics in color. One of those comics was about life in the poorer sections of a big city. It features a boy dressed in a baggy yellow gown. The "Yellow Kid" was an instant success. Hearst seized the opportunity to steal away the comic. He offered the comic's creator a bigger salary, and the artist accepted. The comic moved to the *Journal.* Pulitzer then hired another artist to draw the "Yellow Kid" for his papers. Readers began calling the papers the "yellow kid journals." The phrase became "yellow journalism," which was used to describe sensational stories and headlines.

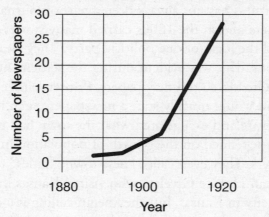

Number of Newspapers Owned by Hearst

The Darkest Shade of Yellow

There is no better example of yellow journalism than the newspapers published immediately before the Spanish-American War. In 1895, corruption and high taxes caused the Cuban people to rebel against their Spanish rulers. The Cubans wanted freedom to run their own country. The Spanish rulers reacted harshly to crush the rebellion. Americans were sympathetic to Cuba, and they closely followed the crisis. America had many financial interests in Cuba, such as sugar and rice plantations. As the rebellion grew, sugar prices dropped, and growers stopped harvesting. Rebels set fire to sugarcane fields.

Headlines in the *World* and the *Journal* screamed for war against Spain. Grisly stories described atrocities in Cuba. The newspapers did their best to excite the public. Public outcry for war grew louder. President William McKinley wanted America to remain neutral. However, when fighting broke out in Havana, he sent the U.S. battleship *Maine* to the Cuban capital city to protect American citizens there. On February 15, 1898, a huge explosion blew apart the ship. Both newspapers stirred up readers' outrage by blaming Spain. The Spanish insisted that they had nothing to do with the explosion. But Americans wanted war. In April 1898, Congress declared war on Spain. It has never been proved that Spainish forces destroyed the *Maine*.

Newspapers Today

Although yellow journalism usually refers to newspapers in the past, readers today must also be wary of bias in all media. Clearly, newspapers have swayed readers' viewpoints on major issues such as the Spanish-American War. Nowadays, readers can also be exposed to bias on television news shows, blogs, Web sites, and social media sites. What does this mean for you? This means that you need to be wary of what you hear and read. Always confirm the information with a second source. And always—always—be curious about the other side of the story.

7. What is the BEST summary of the passage?

A. The term "yellow journalism" came from the phrase "yellow kid journalism." This phrase was used to describe the *Journal* and the *World,* which both printed the "Yellow Kid" cartoon as well as sensational articles.

B. Throughout most of our nation's history, we have gotten our news through newspapers. And in the 1800s, newspapers were known to wildly exaggerate information about towns and cities.

C. Newpapers can be very influential. For example, in the 1800s, certain newspapers tried to get readers angry at Spain, which may have eventually led to the Spanish-American War.

D. Throughout our nation's history, newspapers have been important. Unfortunately, there have been many cases of sensational articles and yellow journalism, so readers need to consider what they read carefully.

8. Which of the following is an example of an opinion from the passage?

A. "It is also important to understand the difference between fact and opinion and to be able to detect bias."

B. "The phrase became 'yellow journalism,' which was used to describe sensational stories and headlines."

C. "He offered the comic's creator a bigger salary, and the artist accepted."

D. "President William McKinley wanted America to remain neutral."

9. Which of the following BEST explains the type of source that this passage represents?

A. This is a primary source because it contains direct quotes from both Horace Greeley and Joseph Pulitzer.

B. This is a primary source because it contains a lot of facts and information about events that happened in the past.

C. This is a secondary source because it tells facts and details about many people.

D. This is a secondary source because the author did not experience all these events and used information from other sources.

10. Read these sentences from the passage.

> **Most reporters try not to show bias. They attempt to give their readers or viewers fair, <u>objective</u> information.**

Based on the context clues, what is the meaning of <u>objective</u>?

A. a topic

B. a goal

C. not influenced by personal feelings

D. a grammatical case, describing a noun

11. Based on the line graph, when did Hearst own the fewest newspapers?

A. 1887

B. 1895

C. 1904

D. 1925

12. What opinion would Horace Greeley MOST LIKELY have had about the yellow journalism connected to the Spanish-American War? Support your answer with details from the passage.

_____

_____

_____

_____

_____

_____

Read the poem and answer the questions that follow.

On the Grasshopper and the Cricket
by John Keats

The poetry of earth is never dead:
    When all the birds are faint with the hot sun,
    And hide in cooling trees, a voice will run
From hedge to hedge about the new-mown mead;
5   That is the Grasshopper's—he takes the lead
    In summer luxury,—he has never done
    With his delights; for when tired out with fun
He rests at east beneath some pleasant weed.
The poetry of earth is ceasing never:
10   On a lone winter evening, when the frost
      Has wrought a silence, from the stove there shrills
The Cricket's song, in warmth increasing ever,
    And seems to one in drowsiness half lost,
      The Grasshopper's among some grassy hills.

13. "On the Grasshopper and the Cricket" is an example of a

    A. lyric poem.

    B. free verse poem.

    C. haiku.

    D. limerick.

14. Read these lines from the poem.

> **The poetry of earth is ceasing**
> **   never:**
> **   On a lone winter evening,**
> **   when the frost**
> **   Has wrought a silence, from**
> **   the stove there shrills**
> **The Cricket's song, in warmth**
> **   increasing ever,**

The poet uses these lines to

    A. encourage readers to listen for crickets.

    B. suggest to readers that the cricket's song is poetry.

    C. compare the sound of the grasshopper to the sound of the cricket.

    D. explain to readers how warm temperatures affect the cricket.

15. Which of the following BEST describes the mood of the poem?

    A. sorrow

    B. passion

    C. happiness

    D. uncertainty

16. Read this line from the poem.

> **The poetry of earth is never dead:**

The poet uses the phrase "the poetry of earth" to mean

    A. the lovely sounds of nature.

    B. the different seasons.

    C. the poems that writers have written.

    D. the songs sung by birds.

17. In line 2, the poet writes "all the birds are faint with the hot sun" to

   A. inform readers about how birds act in the summer.

   B. imply that the birds might never sing again.

   C. show readers that birds can faint just like humans do.

   D. suggest that the heat has stopped the birds from singing.

18. What is the rhyme scheme of "On the Grasshopper and the Cricket"?

   _____

   _____

   _____

   _____

Read the poem and answer the questions that follow.

The Seedling

by Paul Laurence Dunbar

As a quiet little seedling
    Lay within its darksome bed,
To itself it fell a-talking,
    And this is what it said:

5   "I am not so very robust,
    But I'll do the best I can;"
And the seedling from that moment
    Its work of life began.

So it pushed a little leaflet
10   Up into the light of day,
To examine the surroundings
    And show the rest the way.

The leaflet liked the prospect,
    So it called its brother, Stem;
15   Then two other leaflets heard it,
    And quickly followed them.

To be sure, the haste and hurry
    Made the seedling sweat and pant;
But almost before it knew it
20   It found itself a plant.

The sunshine poured upon it,
    And the clouds they gave a shower;
And the little plant kept growing
    Till it found itself a flower.

25   Little folks, be like the seedling,
        Always do the best you can;
    Every child must share life's labor
        Just as well as every man.

    And the sun and showers will help you
30   Through the lonesome, struggling hours,
    Till you raise to light and beauty
        Virtue's fair, unfading flowers.

19. What does the seedling symbolize in the poem?

   A. nature

   B. a teacher

   C. death

   D. a child

20. Which of the following BEST describes the mood of the poem?

   A. hope

   B. excitement

   C. worry

   D. curiosity

21. Read this line from the poem.

   Made the seedling sweat and pant;

   The poet includes this detail to

   A. explain to readers why a seedling sweats.

   B. suggest that the seedling will be unable to grow.

   C. show how growing was work for the seedling.

   D. encourage readers to listen to plants breathe.

22. Read these lines from the poem.

   To itself it fell a-talking,
   And this is what it said:
   "I am not so very robust,
   But I'll do the best I can;"

   The poet uses these lines to

   A. make readers believe that the seedling was really talking.

   B. prove to readers that the author has a wild imagination.

   C. help readers relate to the experiences of the seedling.

   D. persuade readers to talk to themselves when working.

Use "On the Grasshopper and the Cricket" and "The Seedling" to answer questions 23–24.

23. Which statement about the poems is true?

    A. "On the Grasshopper and the Cricket" is a sonnet, whereas "The Seedling" is not.

    B. "On the Grasshopper and the Cricket" is an epic poem, whereas "The Seedling" is not.

    C. "On the Grasshopper and the Cricket" and "The Seedling" have the same rhyme scheme.

    D. "On the Grasshopper and the Cricket" and "The Seedling" have the same number of stanzas.

24. Compare how the poets used rhyme in the poems. Use details from the poems to support your answer.

    _____

    _____

    _____

    _____

    _____

    _____

Part 2: Language Arts

This passage contains mistakes. Read the passage and answer the questions that follow.

Do You Know What's in Your Food?

(1) For many years, scientists have studied the effects of certain chemicals in our foods. (2) Sometimes, as a result, certain chemicals to be banned by the government. (3) For example, you might be familiar with the bottles of food coloring you've used to dye frosting when making cookies. (4) But food <u>coloring</u> is used in many things, such as candies, cereals, lipstick, and more. (5) In the 1970s, the U.S. Food and Drug Administration (FDA) banned red dye no. 2. (6) Later, in 1990, the FDA banned the use of red dye no. 3 in certain foods because studies showed that huge quantities of this dye could cause cancer.

(7) Over the past few years, many people have claimed that there is also a problem with red dye no. 40. (8) Some parents claim that their children's behavior improved after the parents limited the amount of red dye no. 40 in their diets. (9) Specifically, some parents have noted a decline in their children's <u>hyperactivity</u>. (10) This dye is currently banned throughout much of Europe.

(11) Recently, a group of scientists conducted a formal study. (12) They tested the effects of a diet containing various artificial food colorings, including red dye no. 40, on groups of children. (13) You might be amazed by what the scientists found. (14) Their data showed that the presence of artificial food coloring in the children's diet was linked to a statistically significant increase in hyperactivity.

(15) At present, the U.S. government does not appear to have plans to ban red dye no. 40 or other artificial food colorings. (16) But many people don't feel like waiting for the government to act. (17) They have decided to limit their intake on their own. (18) If you have any interest in doing so, you can! (19) First, read the ingredients on the packages of all your food. (20) Second, avoid those foods that contain artificial colorings. (21) Third, buy foods that are made with natural colorings. (22) Companies can make food yellow by using the saffron plant or red by using the juice of elderberries. (23) These sorts of natural colorings can be purchased by your parent or guardian online or in specialty stores.

(24) So, the next time you and your family were wanted to frost some cookies. (25) Consider coloring the frosting naturally.

25. Which of the following corrects the grammar errors in sentence 2?

A. Sometimes, as a result, certain chemicals banned the government.

B. Sometimes, as a result, certain chemicals will ban the government.

C. Sometimes, as a result, certain chemicals have been banned by the government.

D. Sometimes, as a result, certain chemicals are going to ban the government.

26. Read sentence 9.

> **Specifically, some parents have noted a decline in their children's hyperactivity.**

What reference source would BEST help you determine the correct pronunciation of hyperactivity?

A. a magazine

B. an encyclopedia

C. a dictionary

D. a thesaurus

27. Read sentence 4.

> **But food coloring is used in many things, such as candies, cereals, lipstick, and more.**

What is the meaning of the word coloring in this sentence?

A. blushing

B. the act of changing color

C. a substance that changes the color of something

D. making marks with crayons on a piece of paper

28. How should sentences 24 and 25 be edited?

A. So, the next time you and your family want to frost some cookies, consider coloring the frosting naturally.

B. So, the next time you and your family were wanting to frost some cookies, considering color the frosting naturally.

C. So, the next time you and your family were wanting to frost some cookies. Consider coloring the frosting naturally.

D. So, the next time you and your family will be wanting to frost some cookies, consider to color the frosting naturally.

29. Read sentence 19.

First, read the ingredients on the packages of all your food.

How should this sentence be edited to show that the action is only a possibility?

A. First, you should read the ingredients on the packages of all your food.

B. First, you will read the ingredients on the packages of all your food.

C. First, you are reading the ingredients on the packages of all your food.

D. First, you might read the ingredients on the packages of all your food.

30. Read sentence 23.

These sorts of natural colorings can be purchased by your parent or guardian online or in specialty stores.

On the lines below, rewrite the sentence so that it uses active voice instead of passive voice.

_____

_____

_____

_____

Part 3: Writing

Fictional Narrative Prompt

Think about a problem or conflict you have in your everyday life. Now, imagine how a typical eighth-grade student might deal with that problem one hundred years from now. Write a narrative in which the main character is an eighth-grade student who experiences a familiar problem in a futuristic setting. Describe how the technology of the future could help or hinder the character's attempts to solve his or her problem.

Use the checklist below to help you do your best writing.

Does your narrative

❏ have an engaging introduction?

❏ establish a background and point of view?

❏ organize an event sequence that unfolds naturally and logically?

❏ consider purpose and audience?

❏ use narrative techniques to develop experiences, events, and characters?

❏ use a variety of transitions to convey sequence and show relationships between ideas?

❏ use precise and descriptive language?

❏ have a thoughtful conclusion?

Use the following pages to plan and write your response.

Planning Page

Benchmark Assessment 4

Part 1: Reading Comprehension

Read the passage and answer the questions that follow.

The Nor'easter: Power in the Form of Wind and Water

The word *nor'easter* is based on the word *northeast* and describes a type of powerful storm with winds that blow from a northeasterly direction. When there is a strong nor'easter, it often makes the news because these storms have the potential to wreak havoc and major destruction upon people and their homes.

The Dangers of a Nor'easter

Nor'easters are known for being serious storms. While not every nor'easter is dangerous, some can create serious problems. People have died during severe nor'easters. Nor'easters are known for their snow, ice, and strong winds.

When huge amounts of snow and ice fall on an area, this can create very dangerous situations. People can be trapped inside their homes and apartments. Roads become slick, causing deadly car accidents. Planes must be grounded. In some places, it can be difficult for people to get enough water and heat inside their homes because the cold temperatures freeze their pipes.

But perhaps even more deadly are the winds. Some nor'easters have winds as powerful as the winds in a hurricane. The winds can knock down electrical lines and damage homes. In addition, such winds over the ocean cause massive tides. Waters can rise near coasts, flooding towns and eroding the ground under buildings.

What Causes a Nor'easter?

A nor'easter is a type of storm in which the winds move in a spinning direction. This happens because two air currents collide: an air current from the Arctic and an air current from the Gulf of Mexico.

The air current from the Arctic is cold air, which moves from Canada across the United States southeastward toward the Atlantic Ocean. You can think of this air current as moving like the hands of a clock—in other words, in a clockwise direction. This is a high <u>pressure</u> system.

Simultaneously, warm air from around the Gulf of Mexico moves northward. You can think of this air current as moving in the opposite direction of the hands of a clock—in other words, in a counterclockwise direction. This is a low pressure system.

Both of these are natural air currents. When these two very different air currents collide, they create a spinning mix of powerful winds. These two winds mix to form a powerful storm.

Luckily, nor'easters are only common in the cooler months, between October and April. A typical nor'easter might form near the coast of a southeastern state, such as Florida or Georgia. Then it will probably move northeast along the Atlantic coast.

How Does a Nor'easter Form?

Most nor'easters form in the following way:

Step 1: Cold air moves southeastward from the Arctic in a high pressure system.

Step 2: A low pressure system forms around the Gulf of Mexico and moves northeastward.

Step 3: The two air currents meet and collide.

Step 4: The air currents now begin to move northeastward.

Step 5: The air currents gather moisture from the ocean and move this moisture over land.

Step 6: The colder temperatures in the air currents cool the moisture, creating snow and ice.

Step 7: The snow, ice, and winds affect people, buildings, homes, and other property.

Step 8: The storm moves up the Atlantic coastline, sometimes becoming more powerful and sometimes eventually petering out.

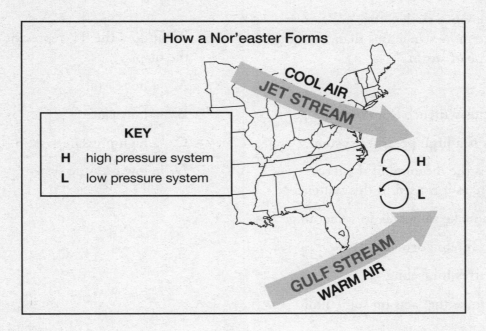

What Ends a Nor'easter?

Nor'easters do eventually end. But how? There are a few ways. Eventually, such storms can lose power, and the winds will die down. Sometimes, a storm will also weaken when it has been traveling over land for a while, as it can no longer gather moisture from the ocean when it is over land. But sometimes, storms continue to be fairly strong and move all the way up the East Coast. Then, they move back into the ocean.

1. The author MOST LIKELY wrote this passage to

   A. explain how nor'easters develop and can affect people and places on land.

   B. persuade readers to live in areas that are not affected by nor'easters.

   C. entertain readers with a wild and intense story about people caught in a storm.

   D. convince readers that nor'easters are more dangerous than any other type of storm.

2. Read this sentence from the passage.

   This is a high <u>pressure</u> system.

   What is the meaning of the term <u>pressure</u> as it is used in this sentence?

   A. to make someone do something

   B. an intense demand

   C. a stressful feeling

   D. a force that acts on something

3. What happens in the formation of a nor'easter before the storm moves in a northeastward direction?

   A. The storm creates snow and ice.

   B. Two air currents meet and collide.

   C. Snow, ice, and winds affect people and their property.

   D. The storm moves up the Atlantic coastline.

4. What does the 'H' represent on the map?

   A. a nor'easter

   B. a hurricane

   C. a high pressure system

   D. a low pressure system

5. What happens after a nor'easter's air currents gather moisture from the ocean?

   A. A low pressure system forms around the Gulf of Mexico.

   B. The two air currents meet and collide.

   C. Cold air from the Arctic moves southeastward.

   D. The colder temperatures in the air currents cool the moisture, creating snow and ice.

6. What are similarities of and differences between the sections "What Causes a Nor'easter?" and "How Does a Nor'easter Form?" Use details from the passage to support your answer.

   _____

   _____

   _____

   _____

   _____

   _____

Read the passage and answer the questions that follow.

Take Care with a Storm Care Kit!

Some studies have shown that the intensity of various types of storms has increased in recent years. Some scientists speculate that this could be due to global warming, while other scientists are unsure of the explanation.

No matter what the reason, the studies suggest that there are more destructive and longer storms happening nowadays.

So, how can you prepare? Most experts recommend that you make yourself a storm preparation kit, so that you can be ready to take care of yourself and your loved ones if a storm, such as a nor'easter, should hit. Find a strong bag or piece of luggage to use as your kit. Then, store the following supplies in your kit somewhere in your home where the kit would be easy to find in case of emergencies. To make a storm preparation kit, you will need the following:

- **Water:** Gather about three days worth of water per person. A person needs about one gallon of water each day, so that means about three gallons of water per person.

- **Food:** Choose food that can be stored without spoiling, such as canned foods. Be sure that all the packages seal tightly and are waterproof. Store three days worth of food per person. You might choose canned beans, canned meats, and so on. Also, pack a can opener and eating utensils.

- **First Aid Kit, Medicine, and Basic Hygiene Items:** Your first aid kit should contain peroxide, bandages, and gauze. If you and/or family members take any regular medication, then pack three to five days worth. People who suffer from certain illnesses, such as diabetes or asthma, will desperately need their medications on a daily basis during an emergency. In addition, you should pack over-the-counter medications, such as cold medicine, cough drops, and painkillers, that are likely to be needed in a storm.

  You might think that the items mentioned above are enough to maintain a basic level of health during an emergency. But often we take things for granted. During a severe storm, such as a nor'easter, there is a chance that you will not have access to soap or hot water. It is important to stay clean so that you do not contract a disease or pass one on to others. Therefore, also pack moisture wipes, antibacterial gel, and toilet paper.

- **Basic Survival Tools:** During a severe storm, the chances increase that the power to your home could go out. You don't want to be caught in the dark, so be sure to pack at least one flashlight with good batteries as well as back-up batteries.

  In addition, without electricity, you and your loved ones will have limited ability to check the news. So, pack a small battery-operated radio. Again, be sure it contains good batteries, and pack a back-up set of batteries. It will be vital for you to find out the status of the storm, rescue crews, and whether or not the storm has passed.

- **Important Documents:** Pack identification for each family member. This should include a social security card, a driver's license, and/or other picture I.D. In addition, pack copies of everyone's medical insurance cards and documents stating any pertinent medical histories. Hopefully, you will not need to use these documents. But if the worst should happen—if your family is evacuated or if someone is seriously injured—then these documents will be vital! Be sure to pack them in a watertight container so that they are not damaged.

- **Cash:** During a serious storm, most banks will be closed, and some ATMs might not work. So, pack enough cash, in small bills, to pay for any basic necessities you might need. For example, you might need to buy additional groceries, refill the family car with gas, or buy bus tickets to travel to a safe destination.

- **Pet Care:** Don't forget the family pet when you're preparing the storm preparation kit! Your pet has needs, too! Review all the items on this list, and pack your pet's version of them. For example, pack water, food, and medication for your pet. Also, be sure that your pet has a collar with a tag that tells people how to reach you in case your pet gets lost in the storm.

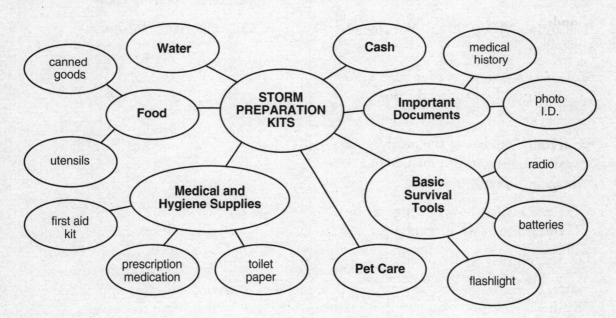

7. The author uses many types of evidence in the passage. Which of the following is an example of research results?

    A. "Some scientists speculate that this could be due to global warming"

    B. "During a severe storm, the chances increase that the power to your home could go out."

    C. "Most experts recommend that you make yourself a storm preparation kit, so that you can be ready"

    D. "Some studies have shown that the intensity of various types of storms has increased in recent years."

8. The author MOST LIKELY included the web to

    A. encourage readers to make a kit that exactly matches the one in the passage.

    B. remind readers of the most important items to include in a storm preparation kit.

    C. show readers how much water is needed for a whole family.

    D. suggest that readers need to put documents in a waterproof container.

9. How does the author structure this passage?

    A. chronological order

    B. compare and contrast

    C. cause and effect

    D. problem and solution

10. According to the passage, to which circle in the web should "antibacterial gel" be connected?

    A. Storm Preparation Kit

    B. Medical and Hygiene Supplies

    C. Basic Survival Tools

    D. Important Documents

Use "The Nor'easter: Power in the Form of Wind and Water" and "Take Care with a Storm Care Kit!" to answer questions 11–12.

11. Both authors include details that show how a nor'easter

    A. can create dangerous situations for people.

    B. often forms near the Gulf of Mexico.

    C. has winds stronger than the winds of a hurricane.

    D. only happens in the middle of winter.

12. What is the main idea of both passages, and how are their main ideas similar and different? Use details from the passages to support your answer.

_____

_____

_____

_____

_____

_____

Read the passage and answer the questions that follow.

Sacagawea Saves the Day

The young woman sat quietly near the back of the boat with her baby strapped to her back in a cradleboard. *Sweet little Pomp*, she thought. The name meant "first born" in her first language. His father insisted on calling him Jean-Baptiste, but Sacagawea knew that her son would always be more Shoshone than French. He was such a good child, just three months old and already a contented traveler.

Sacagawea looked back at her husband Charbonneau. *The Frenchman was hard to live with*, she thought, *but where would she be now if they hadn't married*? Without a doubt, she would be back at the Hidatsa village, where she had spent the last five years since a Hidatsa raiding party had captured her and taken her on a long journey away from her people.

Instead, she and Charbonneau were traveling west with the white men, who said they were going all the way to the big water. They had told Charbonneau that they hoped to find Shoshone and trade with them for horses. They would need horses to take them over the high mountains before the snows came. They thought Sacagawea could help them talk with her people. Well, she would be happy to do that for a chance to see her friends and family again.

Charbonneau had hold of the stick that steered the boat while the rowers and the wind in the sail moved it forward. The two leaders were on the shore watching the boat's progress. The one they called Lewis never had much to say to her. But the other one, Clark, with the hair like flames, smiled often, called her boy "Pompey," and had even given her a nickname. Janey, he called her. She didn't know why. He just seemed glad to have her in the party of thirty-three men.

They should be very glad I am here, Sacagawea thought. These men were helpless when it came to finding food in the woods. They overlooked the most obvious roots and stalks. Already, they had been pleased with the tasty treats she had unearthed.

A sudden chill came over Sacagawea and interrupted her thoughts. The sky had darkened, and the wind was whipping the river into whitecaps. She glanced back at Charbonneau. He looked frightened, but then he was always nervous on the water. She was glad that Cruzatte was in the boat. At least he knew what he was doing.

Suddenly, the wind turned the boat. They were headed toward the shore now, and everyone was shouting at once. In an instant, the boat was on its side, and water was pouring in. It was three hundred yards to the shore. Could she fight the current with Pomp on her back? No, better to stay with the boat.

Charbonneau let go of the steering stick and raised his hands to the sky. Fear was in his eyes. "Why can't he figure out how to save himself and the rest of them?" thought Sacagawea.

Cruzatte, his eyes blazing, was shouting at Charbonneau. Sacagawea didn't know what Cruzatte said, but he must have scared her husband more than the water did because the terrified man had grabbed the steering stick again.

Sacagawea looked around. Bundles of supplies, books, and instruments were floating in the water. Lewis and Clark treasured those things. She had seen them pore over the pages with unfamiliar markings and pictures of the night sky. She had watched them consult their instruments before setting off in a certain direction to hunt.

Without a moment's hesitation, she reached out and grabbed the nearest bundle. The cradleboard shifted on her back, throwing her off balance, but she knew Pomp was secure in it. She struggled with the bundle and got it into the boat. Another package floated nearby. Again, she reached out. Over and over, she pulled the precious bundles out of the water.

Finally, the boat began to right itself. Following Cruzatte's instructions, Charbonneau had managed to get it under control. Cruzatte ordered two men to start bailing while he and two others rowed toward the shore. Sacagawea continued to pluck packages out of the water. In this fashion, the boat pulled up to the shore, barely afloat.

Captain Lewis, who had witnessed the mishap from where he stood on shore, looked happier than she had ever seen him. With much gratitude, he gave her a hand out of the boat before turning to scold Charbonneau.

It was Clark who relieved the tension.

"Janey," he said, "you have saved the day." And he gave her a big grin.

13. Which of the following BEST describes Sacagawea?

A. nervous

B. helpful

C. talkative

D. disappointed

14. What is the point of view of the passage?

A. first person

B. second person

C. third person, limited

D. third person, omniscient

15. Which of the following details BEST supports the idea that the men might have starved without Sacagawea's help?

A. "They would need horses to take them over the high mountains before the snows came."

B. "These men were helpless when it came to finding food in the woods."

C. "Bundles of supplies, books, and instruments were floating in the water."

D. "He was such a good child, just three months old and already a contented traveler."

16. Which event in the passage is part of the rising action?

A. Sacagawea pulls out the last package from the water.

B. Captain Lewis scolds Charbonneau.

C. The sky suddenly darkened.

D. The boat finally made it to shore.

17. Sacagawea would BEST be described as a

    A. trickster.

    B. magic helper.

    C. villain.

    D. hero.

18. What is the theme of the passage? Use details from the passage to support your answer.

_____

_____

_____

_____

_____

_____

For a Robotic Moon Base

Over the years, NASA has studied the moon in various ways: through orbiting satellites and even by astronauts landing on the moon! But some scientists have considered the option of building a base on the moon. This would be a permanent station on the surface of the moon, which would allow scientists to gather even more information.

What Model Should Be Used?

Years ago, scientists built a permanent station in the icy region of Antarctica. Since we've already had this experience, it makes sense to use the Antarctica base to model a moon base in certain ways. For example, at first, several countries claimed those parts of Antarctica that they explored. However, over time, those countries agreed to share. And in 1959, they wisely agreed to collaborate and avoid individual claims to parts of Antarctica.

Since then, Antarctica became a continent without countries. It is open to all countries for scientific work, but no country may take its resources, build a military base, or put weapons there. Our moon base should be similar. It should be a cooperative effort of all the countries of Earth. All countries should be given the right to join if they wish to. The moon should be set aside as a preserve. No country should be allowed to claim any part of it. Like Antarctica, the moon should be open to all countries for peaceful work.

For Which Purpose?

A permanent moon base would offer great opportunities for scientists to study outer space. For one thing, telescopes built at a moon base would be much more powerful than telescopes that are put into orbit. Telescopes launched into space can have fragile parts altered, moved, or broken as a result of being launched. A telescope built on the moon would not have to survive a space launch; therefore, a telescope built on the moon could be more complex.

Source: NASA

In addition, the moon's gravity is much weaker than Earth's gravity. Space vehicles launched from the moon could be smaller, lighter, and more cost-effective than those launched from Earth. That means that space vehicles could be launched from the moon to travel to other planets, such as Mars or Venus, for less money than if they were launched from the surface of Earth.

Why Permanent?

Today, our space program is costly. This is due to many factors. Building advanced technology such as a space shuttle is a very costly process. In addition, sometimes a rocket is used for a single trip and then discarded—never to be used again! We launch a satellite into orbit and then allow it to burn up on re-entry. NASA's current practices are wasteful. In the long run, permanent equipment is cheaper than temporary equipment. A permanent base would make better use of our resources, our energies, and our money. A permanent base can grow, expand, and improve over time.

Why Robots?

Not only should we build a permanent base on the moon, but it should be installed with a plethora of robotic equipment. Yes, granted, some human scientists would be necessary to manage and maintain the robotic equipment and moon station. But overall, having a supply of robotic equipment on a moon base may be more important than having a lot of human astronauts.

First of all, it is easier to send a machine out into space than a human. A machine doesn't need an oxygen supply and can roam over difficult terrain better than a human astronaut can do in a space suit. Second, machines can be used under very harsh conditions, such as in sub-zero freezing temperature—whereas such conditions can pose a real threat to human astronauts. Lastly, all human astronauts must eventually return home. This is due to many factors. Astronauts can develop health issues in space, or they may want to return to see their family. No matter what, a prolonged stay in space wears on the human body. On the other hand, machines can operate in space for very long periods of time. When NASA sent the robotic explorers Spirit and Opportunity to Mars in 2003, they were expected to survive ninety days. More than six years later, these helpful robots were still sending useful data back to Earth. A human mission may do some things that a robotic one cannot, but outlasting its planned stay is not one of them.

All in all, establishing a permanent international robotic base on the moon seems to be a logical course of action. Humans can maintain the base and analyze the data brought back by advanced machines. Such a well-organized base will surely result in major scientific discoveries!

19. Which of the following details is an example of bias?

A. "Years ago, scientists built a permanent station in the icy region of Antarctica."

B. "Building advanced technology such as a space shuttle is a very costly process."

C. "In addition, the moon's gravity is much weaker than Earth's gravity."

D. "And in 1959, they wisely agreed to collaborate and avoid individual claims to parts of Antarctica."

20. Read these sentences from the passage.

> **We launch a satellite into orbit and then allow it to burn up on re-entry. NASA's current practices are wasteful.**

Which of the following BEST explains the type of persuasive technique the author used in these sentences?

A. name-calling

B. testimonial

C. generalization

D. bandwagon

21. In what way does this passage contain incomplete information?

A. The author does not provide any data about the cost or time involved in building a moon base.

B. The author does not explain how a moon base would decrease the costs of space exploration.

C. The author does not say who would live on the moon base.

D. The author does not support his opinion with facts.

22. Read this sentence from the passage.

> **When NASA sent the robotic explorers Spirit and Opportunity to Mars in 2003, they were expected to survive ninety days.**

This is an example of a(n)

A. anecdote.

B. direct quotation.

C. expert opinion.

D. testimonial.

23. Which of the following BEST identifies the author's point of view in the passage?

   A. "Building advanced technology such as a space shuttle is a very costly process."

   B. "All in all, establishing a permanent international robotic base on the moon seems to be a logical course of action."

   C. "A human mission may do some things that a robotic one cannot, but outlasting its planned stay is not one of them."

   D. "For one thing, telescopes built at a moon base would be much more powerful"

24. Write an opposing claim to the one presented in the passage, stating an opinion against building a permanent robotic moon base. Use details to support your argument.

_____

_____

_____

_____

_____

_____

_____

_____

Part 2: Language Arts

This passage contains mistakes. Read the passage and answer the questions that follow.

Real Respect

(1) The term "hazing" is used to describe an activity in which a group of people demand that a person act in a dangerous or <u>embarasing</u> way in order to be accepted into the group. (2) You may have seen representations of hazing in movies featuring college students who are pledging sororities or fraternities. (3) In the movies, the pledges are asked to do embarrassing things, such as running across campus naked or eating a live goldfish. (4) But in real life, hazing isn't funny. (5) There have been many cases of hazing causing serious injuries and even death.

(6) There are countless examples. (7) But to give a face to the problem, consider the case of Matthew Carrington, who died during hazing at a university in California. (8) He was pledging a fraternity. (9) As part of the hazing ritual, he was told to do exercises in extreme circumstances. (10) After hours of this, he collapsing. (11) But initially, his would-be fraternity brothers did nothing. (12) Even after they eventually called an ambulance, none of the fraternity brothers went to the hospital with him. (13) Within a few hours, he passed away. (14) Afterward, several members of the fraternity tried and be found guilty of his death.

(15) Now, several states have passed laws against hazing, and people caught hazing can be charged with a crime. (16) Nonetheless, hazing has continued and even spread. (17) Whereas it used to be found primarily on college campuses, it can now even be found in high schools. (18) A case of this happened recently in Georgia. (19) The marching bands at multiple high schools in Georgia are being investigated for instances of hazing. (20) This stems from a few brutal incidents involving band members who were trying to join a special club, formed by a few members within a marching band. (21) As a result of hazing, one student was beaten and another student died.

(22) Because of the seriousness of the problem, school administrators and other adults are asking students everywhere to help. (23) Students who know about or have seen hazing are encouraged to report it. (24) Often, students can even report hazing anonymously.

(25) While groups that secretly conduct hazing often describe it as a way for new members to "earn respect," students everywhere should deeply consider what "respect" really means. (26) Being asked to humiliate yourself, endure injuries, or risk death is not respect. (27) Speaking up for yourself or on behalf of your friends—now that shows real respect.

25. How should sentence 10 be edited?

   A. After hours of this, he is collapsing.

   B. After hours of this, he collapsed.

   C. After hours of this, he will collapse.

   D. After hours of this, he collapse.

26. Read sentences 3 and 4.

> **In the movies, the pledges are asked to do embarrassing things, such running across campus naked or eating a live goldfish. But in real life, hazing isn't funny.**

How should these sentences be rewritten in order to show that certain words have been omitted?

   A. In the movies, the pledges are asked to do embarrassing things. But in real life, hazing isn't funny.

   B. In the movies, the pledges are asked to do embarrassing things. But in real life, hazing isn't funny.

   C. In the movies, the pledges are asked to do embarrassing things—in real life, hazing isn't funny.

   D. In the movies, the pledges are asked to do embarrassing things… But in real life, hazing isn't funny.

27. What is the correct spelling of the word <u>embarasing</u>?

   A. embarrasing

   B. embarassing

   C. embbarasing

   D. embarrassing

28. Read sentence 23.

> **Students who know about or have seen hazing are encouraged to report it.**

How could this sentence be revised to create a more serious and urgent mood?

   A. Students who know about or have seen hazing are asked to report it.

   B. Students who know about or have seen hazing must report it immediately.

   C. Students who know about or have seen hazing are recommended to report it.

   D. Students who know about or have seen hazing are invited to report it.

29. What is the BEST way to combine sentences 8 and 9?

A. He was pledging a fraternity, because as part of the hazing ritual, he was told to do exercises in extreme circumstances.

B. He was pledging a fraternity, although as part of the hazing ritual, he was told to do exercises in extreme circumstances.

C. He was pledging a fraternity, and as part of the hazing ritual, he was told to do exercises in extreme circumstances.

D. He was pledging a fraternity, despite part of the hazing ritual, he was told to do exercises in extreme circumstances.

30. Read sentence 14.

Afterward, several members of the fraternity tried and be found guilty of his death.

Some verbs in this sentence are not in the correct voice. Revise this sentence on the lines below.

_____

_____

_____

_____

Part 3: Writing

Persuasive Writing Prompt

Over the past twenty years, computer technology has become an important part of everyday life for much of the global population. Some people view the Internet as a significant means of communication that enhances our knowledge of the world and each other. Others think that our reliance on technology is damaging our ability to engage with people in real life. Is the Internet ultimately helpful or harmful to our social relationships? Support your argument with details and experiences from your own life.

Use the checklist below to help you do your best writing.

Does your essay

❏ clearly introduce a claim?

❏ support the claim with relevant reasoning and evidence?

❏ have a logical organization?

❏ demonstrate an understanding of the topic?

❏ show relationships among ideas?

❏ maintain a formal style?

❏ provide an appropriate conclusion for the argument?

❏ consider purpose and audience?

Use the following pages to plan and write your response.

Planning Page

Summative Assessment

Part 1: Reading Comprehension

Read the passage and answer the questions that follow.

Bridge to Bravery

Cindy stood in a parking lot with her new friend Leya, Leya's grandmother, and about fifteen tourists waiting to walk across the Golden Gate Bridge in San Francisco, California. Cindy read the plaque on the statue of Joseph Strauss, "The Man Who Built the Bridge."

"I wish you had *not* built the bridge," Cindy joked to herself. But behind her joke, Cindy was secretly worried. She'd never liked heights. Just then, the tour guide enthusiastically announced, "Welcome to our tour. You are going to learn about this remarkable bridge that is suspended 240 feet above the Golden Gate." Cindy rolled her eyes. She couldn't believe someone could be so relaxed and happy about being 240 feet in the air. "Why did I get myself into this?" she thought, knowing the answer.

Her family had moved to San Francisco in March. While transferring to a new school late in the year sounded like a bad idea to her, the students at her new school had been friendly. She'd made a few friends fairly quickly.

Leya was the student with whom Cindy hung out the most. Several days earlier, while they ate their lunches in the school cafeteria, Leya had told Cindy that her grandmother was coming to the city to do some sightseeing, now that the weather was getting nice. "Since you are new to the city, why don't you join us?" Leya had suggested. Cindy had thought that sightseeing sounded like a fun way to spend a Saturday, not realizing that the day would include a tour of a bridge.

"You'll want to put on your jackets because the wind is gusty on the bridge," the guide suggested. Cindy realized that the guide was just trying to be kind and helpful, but all it did was make her more nervous. Images of wind gusts blowing them off the bridge started to flood her mind.

The guide noticed Cindy's concern, and added, "I promise we won't experience anything like the seventy-mile-per-hour wind that blasted the bridge on December 1, 1951. The bridge swayed twenty-four feet from side to side then. But as you can see, it's still here!" he joked.

That was not the kind of joke Cindy wanted to hear. Suddenly, she desperately wanted to leave. Then she thought, "I can't make Leya and her grandmother miss the tour just because I'm scared. I'll have to get through this somehow." Cindy took a deep breath and followed Leya onto the bridge, noticing with relief that the pedestrian walkway was about ten feet wide. She positioned herself on the side away from the water, but her heart was still pounding.

Cindy ignored the guide's talk as she attempted to coach herself through her fear. She discovered that looking straight ahead helped. She could almost imagine she was on a regular street as the noisy traffic bustled by.

Cindy noticed the tour guide pointing at the cables as he explained that the Golden Gate is a suspension bridge. "Its cables have a diameter of thirty-six and half inches," he informed the group. Somehow, that information was comforting to Cindy. The guide commented that bridges suspended on cables were not a new idea. "Originally, bridge cables were made of vines, by the fourth century, of braided bamboo."

"Well, I guess things could be worse," Cindy thought. She relaxed a little. Her heart had stopped pounding, and her stomach felt better. She chanced glancing down at the water and then said to Leya, "The windsurfers down there look like miniature dolls."

Cindy found that she had relaxed enough to listen to the guide's comments. After talking about the dimensions of the bridge, he stated, "Maintaining and painting the bridge is a gigantic task, but the paint prevents the bridge from corroding."

"I know what job I don't want after I graduate," Cindy joked to Leya. As the girls chuckled, their guide announced, "You have finished your 1.7-mile walk across the Golden Gate Bridge." Cindy couldn't believe that they were on the other side already. Realizing that she had not used the camera hanging around her neck, she turned around and shot a photograph looking up at the towers and cables. She was still a little nervous, but now, looking back at the bridge, she could see how it was also beautiful. "I am going to hang this picture in my room," Cindy smiled and said to Leya.

1. What is the theme of the passage?

   A. It's good to understand your limits.

   B. Always act respectfully toward friends and elders.

   C. Sometimes, things are less scary than they seem.

   D. Don't do anything you don't want to do.

2. What is the point of view of the passage?

   A. first person

   B. second person

   C. third person, limited

   D. third person, omniscient

3. Which of the following details from the passage BEST supports the idea that the Golden Gate Bridge is long?

   A. "As the girls chuckled, their guide announced, 'You have finished your 1.7-mile walk across the Golden Gate Bridge.'"

   B. "'You are going to learn about this remarkable bridge that is suspended 240 feet above the Golden Gate.'"

   C. "'I promise we won't experience anything like the seventy-mile-per-hour wind that blasted the bridge on December 1, 1951.'"

   D. "Cindy took a deep breath and followed Leya onto the bridge, noticing with relief that the pedestrian walkway was about ten feet wide."

4. Which of the following BEST describes Cindy?

   A. calm

   B. resentful

   C. courageous

   D. disappointed

5. When does this passage MOST LIKELY take place?

   A. fall

   B. winter

   C. spring

   D. summer

6. Read this sentence from the passage.

   Images of wind gusts blowing them off the bridge started to flood her mind.

   Explain how the author uses this sentence to create a feeling of suspense. Use details from the passage to support your answer.

   _____

   _____

   _____

   _____

   _____

   _____

Read the poem and answer the questions that follow.

To a Friend
by Amy Lowell

I ask but one thing of you, only one,
    That always you will be my dream of you;
    That never shall I wake to find untrue
All this I have believed and rested on,
5   Forever vanished, like a vision gone
    Out into the night. Alas, how few
    There are who strike in us a chord we knew
Existed, but so seldom heard its tone
    We tremble at the half-forgotten sound.
10   The world is full of rude awakenings
    And heaven-born castles shattered to the ground,
Yet still our human longing vainly clings
    To a belief in beauty through all wrongs.
    O stay your hand, and leave my heart its songs!

7. Which of the following BEST describes the mood of the poem?

   A. anger

   B. relief

   C. amazement

   D. longing

8. "To a Friend" is an example of a(n)

   A. haiku.

   B. free verse poem.

   C. sonnet.

   D. epic poem.

9. Read this excerpt from the poem.

   **…Alas, how few
   There are who strike in us
   a chord we knew
   Existed, but so seldom heard
   its tone**

   The poet uses these words to

   A. suggest that true friends make music together.

   B. encourage readers to listen for music when they meet new people.

   C. explain how the heart can be played like an instrument.

   D. compare the feeling of friendship to a musical note.

10. Read this line from the poem.

    **And heaven-born castles
    shattered to the ground,**

    What do "heaven-born castles" symbolize in the poem?

    A. homes

    B. hopes

    C. clouds

    D. music

11. Read these lines from the poem.

> **I ask but one thing of you, only one,**
> > **That always you will be my dream of you;**
> > **That never shall I wake to find untrue**
> **All this I have believed and rested on,**

The poet uses the phrase "never shall I wake" to mean

A. the speaker gets to sleep late.

B. the friend is only in the speaker's dreams.

C. the speaker's dreams are happier than her real life.

D. the speaker doesn't want her friend to betray her.

12. What is the rhyme scheme of "To a Friend"?

_____

_____

_____

_____

Read the passage and answer the questions that follow.

An Unusual Type of Farm

All over the world, people are building a new type of farm. This type of farm is not intended to grow anything. But it does harvest something special—energy.

A "wind farm" is the term now used to describe a group of wind turbines that have been placed in the same general area to produce energy. Wind farms can be fairly small, containing only a handful of wind turbines, or they can be quite large, with several hundred wind turbines. Another unusual thing about wind farms is that they can be on land or off the coast. As long as the wind turbines are placed in an area that gets a lot of wind, they can produce the electricity we so vitally need around the world.

What Is a Wind Turbine?

A wind turbine is the core component of a wind farm. It is usually constructed out of a strong metal so that it can endure strong winds. Wind turbines contain a few key components: the base (which is shaped like a flag pole), the blades (which often resemble a plane's propellers), and the battery or electrical storage facility (which stores and transports the energy collected by the turbine).

While in the past, wind turbines came in many shapes and sizes, nowadays, wind turbines tend to have three blades. Scientists have found that three-bladed turbines have an efficient and reliable shape for collecting wind power.

Why Use Wind Power?

These turbines somehow produce energy from wind, but how? First of all, as the wind passes over the turbine, it pushes upon the blades, causing them to move. Through this process, the <u>kinetic</u> energy of the wind is transformed into mechanical energy. The movement of the blades is connected to a battery or to an electrical storage facility, which allows the mechanical energy to be transformed into electrical energy.

This electrical energy can be used for anything! It can travel along standard electrical lines to your home, where you can use it to power your TV, game systems, refrigerator, and more, just as you normally would. In your home, you'd have no way to tell the difference between wind power and other power sources.

But the significance of wind power cannot be underestimated. Most of our energy comes from fossil fuel sources, such as coal, which can create significant health and environmental hazards. As you most likely know, all stages of fossil fuel use produces pollution and releases toxins into the environment—from mining for coal, shipping the coal, and processing the coal.

But wind energy doesn't do this. Overall, most scientists consider wind energy to create minimal health or environmental problems. The land can still be used for other things, such as for cattle, farms, or grassland. The turbines require no fuel and produce no toxins or pollutants. Some people living near wind farms have stated that the turbines have killed flying bats and birds, but there is no information yet to show that more animals are killed by flying into a wind turbine than are killed by the destruction of animals' habitats by pollution from fossil fuel production. Meanwhile, many scientists associate the endangering and extinction of some species with human's over-reliance on fossil fuels.

Who Uses Wind Power?

Countries around the world are already using wind power. Presently, the United States is producing the most overall wind energy from wind farms, but China is producing the highest percentage of its overall energy needs through wind farms. By 2030, the United States might be able to produce 20 percent of the nation's overall energy through wind power. But China might be able to produce *all* of its energy by 2030 through wind power.

This is good news! The more countries around the world are able to rely on wind energy, the less we will need to rely on fossil fuels. And that means that countries around the world could produce far less carbon dioxide emissions. This is significant, as carbon dioxide is linked to the greenhouse effect and global warming. As more and more countries realize the disastrous results that global warming could have on land, animals, and people, the pursuit of carbon-emission-free forms of energy becomes even more necessary.

Some critics say that wind power isn't the solution because wind farms can only produce energy when it is windy. For certain areas of the world, this might mean that wind farms produce energy in certain seasons or certain months of the year. But there are solutions to this problem. Countries relying on wind energy can store extra energy created during windy months to be used during less windy seasons. In addition, countries can share their energy.

As countries continue to develop wind farms, they are bound to become more efficient and develop solutions to these concerns. Over time, wind farms could be the solution to our energy concerns, and the world might expect to see a completely carbon-emission-free form of energy.

13. The author MOST LIKELY wrote this passage to

    A. convince readers only to use electricity that has been gathered by wind farms.

    B. entertain readers with fascinating stories of wind farms being built in countries around the world.

    C. inform readers about how wind farms produce wind energy and less pollution than other types of energy sources.

    D. explain to readers why certain types of wind turbines are more efficient than other types.

14. Read this sentence from the passage.

    Through this process, the <u>kinetic</u> energy of the wind is transformed into mechanical energy.

    Based on context clues, <u>kinetic</u> MOST LIKELY refers to energy that comes from

    A. motion.

    B. the sun.

    C. water.

    D. electricity.

15. Which of the following is an opinion in the passage?

    A. "But the significance of wind power cannot be underestimated."

    B. "Countries around the world are already using wind power."

    C. "The turbines require no fuel and produce no toxins or pollutants."

    D. "It is usually constructed out of a strong metal so that it can endure strong winds."

16. Which of the following details is an example of an opposing claim?

    A. "Scientists have found that three-bladed turbines have an efficient and reliable shape for collecting wind power."

    B. "Through this process, the kinetic energy of the wind is transformed into mechanical energy."

    C. "Wind farms can be fairly small, containing only a handful of wind turbines, or they can be quite large"

    D. "Some critics say that wind power isn't the solution because wind farms can only produce energy when it is windy."

17. Read this sentence from the passage.

By 2030, the United States might be able to <u>produce</u> 20 percent of the nation's overall energy through wind power.

What is the meaning of the term <u>produce</u> as it is used in this sentence?

A. to make valuable

B. to create

C. fruits or vegetables

D. something that is made

18. What is the main idea of the passage? Use details from the passage to support your answer.

_____

_____

_____

_____

_____

_____

Not in Our Town

There's no denying that we use a lot of electricity. The town of Winthrop lights its roads at night. We air-condition our schools during the hottest school days of the year so that our students may stay focused on their studies. And of course, each of us, as individuals, uses an enormous amount of electricity to simply do the basic day-to-day activities in our homes.

So, I, like many other residents, feel it is incredibly important that we consider a sustainable and healthy source of energy to meet all our needs. Nonetheless, I seriously oppose the proposition to build a wind farm on the outskirts of our town.

Many advocates of building a wind farm in Winthrop are distracted by the promises of pollution-free energy and the idea of modernization, but these ideas do not express the reality of wind farms. I have had the opportunity to see and visit wind farms, and I can express with first hand knowledge the problems that lay in wait. I can summarize the problems in the following words: eyesore, damage to wildlife, and poor output.

First of all, wind farms can be an eyesore. Sure, one or two wind turbines look fine, but it can be hard to really imagine miles and miles of clustered wind turbines. A few years ago, I had the chance to travel around the world, and in some smaller countries, I saw some wind turbines built out of rickety pieces of wood. The turbines practically looked like merry-go-rounds—they were so huge and with so many blades. They blocked the view of the landscape. Here in Winthrop, we are so lucky to have hillsides lush with trees, meandering streams, and wide blue skies. A wind farm would block that view. Many of us chose to live here because of that view, so why would we choose to lose it?

Secondly, wind farms have been known to kill unsuspecting birds that fly into the turbines. Most people know how birds sometimes fly straight into glass windows or glass buildings because they do not realize something is there, and this impact seriously injures or kills the birds. Similarly, the blades of wind turbines can move so quickly that they are a blur. There are reports from people who live near wind farms that birds are being killed because they do not realize there are quickly chopping blades in the sky. I do not think that the energy achieved from wind farms is a fair trade-off for the loss of such crucial wildlife. Birds bring beauty and song to our lives. But they also eat mosquitoes and other insects. If birds disappeared from Winthrop, I think we would all notice their absence and regret it.

Lastly, I am concerned by our town's prediction of the amount of energy that could be created for our community by a wind farm. I would like the assessments of the amount of energy to be double-checked by an outside source. My understanding of wind farms is that the turbines are not able to produce high levels of energy all year round. During my travels, I saw turbines that barely moved! What's the point of them, then? And some turbines are just not that efficient. I wouldn't want our town to invest a lot of money in building wind turbines that, it turns out, are not very efficient and turn very little wind energy into the electricity we need.

I have shared my information with my neighbors. While some people smartly see my point of view, others have told me that my information is outdated. One neighbor pointed out that the fuels we presently use also hinder the natural beauty of our town in that the exhaust and air pollution created from burning fossil fuels can mar the beauty of our natural landscape. I can understand my neighbor's point of view, but I have to insist: Why should we choose any method of getting energy that will create an eyesore? We shouldn't. That means we shouldn't choose to burn fossil fuels that create smog, just as we shouldn't build a wind farm that could block the view of our majestic hillsides.

I believe that another, better option is attainable. Certainly, we as a town can pick an energy source that is not an eyesore, does not damage wildlife in any way, and efficiently produces the energy we need. We just need to pursue a better energy solution. I implore my neighbors and fellow residents: Please think through the decision to build a wind farm. I think another, better option will be right around the corner if we could all just have the patience to wait for it.

19. Which of the following details is an example of bias?

   A. "A few years ago, I had the chance to travel around the world, and in some smaller countries, I saw some wind turbines"

   B. "While some people smartly see my point of view, others have told me that my information is outdated."

   C. "We air-condition our schools during the hottest school days of the year so that our students may stay focused on their studies."

   D. "Similarly, the blades of wind turbines can move so quickly that they are a blur."

20. Read these sentences from the passage.

   During my travels, I saw turbines that barely moved! What's the point of them, then?

   These sentences contain an example of

   A. snob appeal.

   B. qualifying words.

   C. a hasty generalization.

   D. bandwagon appeal.

21. Which of the following BEST identifies the author's point of view in the passage?

   A. "Nonetheless, I seriously oppose the proposition to build a wind farm on the outskirts of our town."

   B. "in some smaller countries, I saw some wind turbines built out of rickety pieces of wood"

   C. "Many advocates of building a wind farm in Winthrop are distracted by the promises of pollution-free energy"

   D. "While some people smartly see my point of view, others have told me that my information is outdated."

22. Read this sentence from the passage.

   There are reports from people who live near wind farms that birds are being killed because they do not realize there are quickly chopping blades in the sky.

   This is an example of a(n)

   A. survey result.

   B. direct quotation.

   C. expert opinion.

   D. anecdote.

Use "An Unusual Type of Farm" and "Not in Our Town" to answer questions 23–24.

23. Which of the following BEST identifies a difference between the passages?

    A. The first passage suggests that birds can be killed by wind turbines, whereas the second passage suggests a solution to this problem.

    B. The first passage states that wind turbines are usually made out of metal, whereas the second passage describes some wind turbines as made out of wood.

    C. The first passage describes energy sources that are better than wind energy, whereas the second passage describes the benefits of wind energy.

    D. The first passage states that wind power can only be used during windy seasons, whereas the second passage suggests a solution to this problem.

24. Compare the two passages. Which passage contains the MOST relevant and sufficient evidence? Use details from the passages to support your answer.

    _____

    _____

    _____

    _____

    _____

    _____

Part 2: Language Arts

This passage contains mistakes. Read the passage and answer the questions that follow.

Volunteer!

(1) Over the past few years, the economy to be talked about a lot. (2) You may have heard about the <u>recession</u> from watching news shows, reading the newspaper, or listening to your family chat about their worries. (3) Sometimes, when unemployment rates are higher, jobs are more difficult to find for older people. (4) But during this past recession, a lot of young graduates also expressed difficulty with finding work. (5) Many young graduates felt thrilled as they completed their high school or college degrees. (6) But this excitement quickly turned to <u>disapointment</u> if they couldn't find a job.

(7) As a result, some teenagers are revising their plans. (8) In the past, most teenagers would typically complete high school with the hopes of successfully completing a college degree or getting a job. (9) Now, some teenagers are considering volunteering.

(10) Most volunteer opportunities are unpaid. (11) But some offer a small payment to workers. (12) Despite this, the benefits can be enormous. (13) First of all, young people have the opportunity to develop real job experiences. (14) Job experience is important to employers. (15) Real job experience can help a new graduate get a job.

(16) Volunteering also helps young people decide if a job is right for them. (17) For example, a teenager could volunteer at a local hospital and at a local veterinary office. (18) The teenager might realize that he or she prefers to work with people. (19) As a result, that teen can more confidently pursue the training needed to become a nurse, doctor, or medical technician. (20) In the long run, this can help people save on college tuition. (21) Instead of taking classes only to learn you don't like the field later, you can have a glimpse into that field by volunteering.

(22) In addition, many young people state that volunteering allows them to make friends and contribute to society in a meaningful way. (23) There are many opportunities around the country and around the world for volunteering, such as the Peace Corps, Habitat for Humanity, AmeriCorps, and Serve.gov.

(24) As First Lady Michelle Obama said, "[E]ach of us—no matter what our age or background or walk of life—each of us has something to contribute to the life of this nation."

25. Read sentence 2.

You may have heard about the <u>recession</u> from watching news shows, reading the newspaper, or listening to your family chat about their worries.

What reference source could you use to find an antonym of <u>recession</u>?

A. a dictionary

B. a glossary

C. an encyclopedia

D. a thesaurus

26. How should sentence 23 be written in order to show that you have deleted certain words?

A. There are many opportunities. Such as the Peace Corps, Habitat for Humanity, AmeriCorps, and Serve.gov.

B. There are many opportunities; such as the Peace Corps, Habitat for Humanity, AmeriCorps, and Serve.gov.

C. There are many opportunities … such as the Peace Corps, Habitat for Humanity, AmeriCorps, and Serve.gov.

D. There are many opportunities, such as the Peace Corps, Habitat for Humanity, AmeriCorps, and Serve.gov.

27. What is the correct spelling of the word <u>disapointment</u>?

A. disappointment

B. dissappointment

C. dissapointment

D. dissapontment

28. Read sentence 1.

Over the past few years, the economy to be talked about a lot.

How should sentence 1 be edited?

A. Over the past few years, the economy will be talked about a lot.

B. Over the past few years, the economy is talking about a lot.

C. Over the past few years, the economy has been talked about a lot.

D. Over the past few years, the economy might talk about a lot.

29. Reread sentence 21.

Instead of taking classes only to learn you don't like the field later, you can have a glimpse into that field by volunteering.

The author used the phrase "to learn" to describe an action that

A. could happen in the future.

B. will definitely happen.

C. is happening right now.

D. happened a long time ago.

30. Read sentences 14 and 15.

Job experience is important to employers. Real job experience can help a new graduate get a job.

Combine these sentences into one sentence on the lines below.

_____

_____

_____

_____

Part 3: Writing

Read the passages and respond to the prompt that follows.

Joseph McCarthy and the Communist Scare
by Sharon Belgrave

On February 9, 1950, Senator Joseph McCarthy gave a reelection speech in which he accused members of the State Department of being Communists or Communist sympathizers. McCarthy wanted power, and feeding America's fear of communism was a way to get it.

The fear of communism grew out of the Cold War power struggle between the Soviet Union and the United States. When McCarthy became chairman of the Senate Permanent Subcommittee on Investigations in 1953, he set up hearings to investigate labor leaders, artists in the film industry, and members of the executive branch of the federal government. Hundreds of people were asked the question, "Are you now or have you ever been a member of the Communist Party?"

Excerpt from a telegram from Senator Joseph McCarthy to President Harry Truman, 1950

WB055 DL PD
RENO NEV FEB 11 1139A
THE PRESIDENT
THE WHITE HOUSE

In a Lincoln Day speech at Wheeling [West Virginia] Thursday night I stated that the State Department harbors a nest of communists and communist sympathizers who are helping to shape our foreign policy. I further stated that I have in my possession the names of 57 communists who are in the State Department at present. A State Department spokesman flatly denied this and claimed that there is not a single communist in the department. You can convince yourself of the falsity [lie] of the State Department claim very easily. You will recall that you personally appointed a board to screen State Department employees for the purpose of weeding out fellow travelers [communists]. Your board did a painstaking job, and named hundreds which it listed as "dangerous to the security of the nation," because of communist connections…

Failure on your part [to take action against the supposed "communists"] will label the Democratic Party of being the bedfellow of international communism. Certainly this label is not deserved by the hundreds of thousands of loyal American Democrats throughout the nation, and by the sizable number of able loyal Democrats in both the Senate and the House.

Joe McCarthy U.S.S. WIS.

Draft of President Harry Truman's Reply

My dear Senator:

I read your telegram of February eleventh from Reno, Nevada, with a great deal of interest and this is the first time in my experience, and I was ten years in the Senate, that I ever heard of a Senator trying to discredit his own Government before the world. You know that isn't done by honest public officials. Your telegram is not only not true but an insolent approach to a situation that should have been worked out between man and man but it shows conclusively that you are not even fit to have a hand in the operation of the Government of the United States.

I am very sure that the people of Wisconsin are extremely sorry that they are represented by a person who has as little sense of responsibility as you have.

Sincerely yours,
HST

The Era of McCarthyism
from A Study of Significant Periods in U.S. History
by Jeffrey Walker and Kaya Amjad

McCarthyism describes an era in U.S. history in which many Americans were terrified that the country and government had been infiltrated by Communists. The era is known for paranoia, false accusations, and public trials conducted without substantial proof or evidence.

At the time—in the late 1930s through the mid-1950s—Americans were concerned that communism could spread to the United States. Communism had gained power in other parts of the world, such as the Soviet Union and China. So to many Americans, it seemed plausible that American democracy could be at risk.

Unfortunately, some officials—Joseph McCarthy, in particular—used these fears to conduct unfair and sometimes unconstitutional actions against the American public. McCarthy targeted artists and actors, for some reason believing they were more likely to be Communists. People he accused or considered to be Communists were "blacklisted," meaning that these actors were no longer hired by major companies to work in movies. People were jailed, simply because they were unwilling to lie and accuse others of being Communists. Many careers were destroyed, yet McCarthy rarely had any hard evidence. Often all he had was a person—who knew he or she would be jailed otherwise—who said that another person was a Communist. The fear and accusations spread like wildfire.

Luckily, some people had the courage to risk their careers and stand up against McCarthyism. Eventually, the Communist Scare lost its momentum. Nowadays, most people look back on this point in history with a sense of shame.

The Life of Joseph McCarthy
by Warren Chu

Joseph McCarthy was born in Wisconsin in 1908. While he left school as a teenager to work as a chicken farmer, he eventually returned to school. He went on to complete a college degree and become a lawyer.

Originally a supporter of the Democratic Party, when McCarthy failed to be nominated as a candidate for district attorney through the party, he chose to switch to the Republican Party.

He was known for his dirty campaign strategies. After a stint with the marines, he became a senator, and his disingenuous campaign tactics continued. Eventually, people started to come forward saying that McCarthy had lied about the extent of his marine record. This may have been what spurred McCarthy to begin his anti-communism campaign. For the next few years, McCarthy investigated supposed Communists in America, and he ran his investigation like a witch hunt.

But frequently the public ended up learning that there was no proof to support McCarthy's accusations against certain people. Eventually, his illegitimate tactics were exposed. Politicians from both parties condemned his conduct. Shortly after, his political career came to an end.

Informative/Explanatory Writing Prompt

In your own words, explain how Senator Joseph McCarthy helped to increase American's fear of communism during the 1940s and 1950s. Then, describe how McCarthyism was eventually discredited. Choose credible facts and details from the resources provided to support your response, appropriately citing your sources.

Use the checklist below to help you do your best writing.

Does your essay

❏ clearly introduce the topic?

❏ have logical organization and formatting?

❏ develop the topic with relevant facts, details, and examples from the sources provided?

❏ correctly cite facts and details from the sources?

❏ use a variety of transitions to show relationships between ideas?

❏ maintain a formal style?

❏ provide an appropriate conclusion?

❏ consider purpose and audience?

Use the following pages to plan and write your response.

Planning Page

Notes

Notes

Notes

Notes

Notes

Notes

Notes

Notes

Notes

Notes

Notes

Notes

Notes

Notes